HEALING FROM LIFE'S DEEPEST HURTS

HEALING
FROM LIFE'S
DEEPEST
HURTS

Reclaiming Your Life After
Grief, Loss, or Trauma

KIMBERLY HAAR,
LPC, LMFT

BakerBooks
a division of Baker Publishing Group
Grand Rapids, Michigan

© 2025 by Kimberly Haar

Published by Baker Books
a division of Baker Publishing Group
Grand Rapids, Michigan
BakerBooks.com

Printed in the United States of America

Library of Congress Cataloging-in-Publication Data

Names: Haar, Kimberly, 1966– author.

Title: Healing from life's deepest hurts : reclaiming your life after grief, loss, or trauma / Kimberly Haar.

Description: Grand Rapids, Michigan : Baker Books, a division of Baker Publishing Group, [2025] | Includes bibliographical references.

Identifiers: LCCN 2024030014 | ISBN 9781540904560 (paper) | ISBN 9781540904959 (casebound) | ISBN 9781493450428 (ebook)

Subjects: LCSH: Grief. | Loss (Psychology) | Psychic trauma.

Classification: LCC BF575.G7 H238 2025 | DDC 155.9/3—dc23/eng/20240905

LC record available at https://lccn.loc.gov/2024030014

25 26 27 28 29 30 31   7 6 5 4 3 2 1

For everything there is a season,
  a time for every activity under heaven.
A time to be born and a time to die.
  A time to plant and a time to harvest.
A time to kill and a time to heal.
  A time to tear down and a time to build up.
A time to cry and a time to laugh.
  A time to grieve and a time to dance.

ECCLESIASTES 3:1–4 NLT

Contents

A Note to the Reader

In this book, I recount how I was once assaulted by my ex-husband. As anyone who has survived an assault or traumatic loss of any kind will understand, the act of taking back your personal power—that is, remembering what is within your control and exercising that control—is an important part of healing. With that in mind, I have chosen to focus my story not on what was done *to* me but rather on what God has done *in* me. I also have made the decision not to refer to my perpetrator by name, aiming to protect all those affected by this tragedy. In addition, I have changed some identifying details of real-life events to protect the privacy of certain individuals.

In chapter 5, I chose to tell my story in a way that intentionally focuses on the healing and hope that happened in the aftermath of the attack. I have made every effort to handle this material carefully to protect readers who may have endured their own trauma. Be aware, however, that the story of my assault does include some details that could be upsetting to sensitive readers.

This story is not about a villain and a victim. Instead, it is about a woman who, despite being victimized, chose healing and emerged victorious. I pray that my story serves as a beacon of hope for you, reminding you that you're not alone in your pain and that, like me, you can not only survive but thrive beyond trauma.

May we all find purpose that can come out of our pain and move forward with courage and resilience.

Introduction

As a licensed counselor, I've had the honor of working with hundreds of women over the past fifteen years as they are on their own journeys and facing unanswered questions. Hour by hour, I've sat with them as they vulnerably pour out their hearts to me, even as they long to hear the words, *I get it! I've felt that way too.* Every woman faces struggles—heartbreaks and trials, worries and losses. In such moments, we long for comfort, hope, even a path to healing.

Maybe that's why I feel like I know you, my friend.

I've seen you in the face of every woman who comes into my office hoping to find relief from her pain. I ask how her week has been, and she answers with "Fine," but her tears tell a different story.

I've seen you in the face of the woman who battles rejection. She recently discovered her husband's affair and now questions the very worth of her soul.

I've seen you in the face of the grieving widow. Feeling lost, she now has the daunting task of beginning a new life alone.

I've seen you in the face of the grown daughter whose father left when she was just a little girl. She continues to wonder why she wasn't enough to make him want to stay.

I've seen you in the face of the mother who prays for her child in addiction. She wrestles with feelings of powerlessness and fear.

And I've seen you in the face of the woman staring at herself in the mirror.

You see, that's because that woman is me.

So hear me when I say, *I get it, and I've felt that way too!*

While our wounds may be different, the questions we ask and the pain we feel are very much the same. We wonder if somehow we "missed" God. Did we mess up so badly somewhere along the way that He cannot (or worse, will not) forgive our mistakes? If we're really honest with ourselves, there are times we even question the very existence of our faith.

How do I know this? Because I'm no different from you.

An Invitation to Dance

In 2017, after surviving a brutal assault and kidnapping, I found myself wrapped in a thick green blanket and lying face down under a pergola nestled among trees as I cried out to God, "Why me?"

Just six days earlier, my entire world had come crashing down around me. In deep pain, I was left staring at the shattered pieces of my life, wondering how or if I would ever be able to put them back together again.

Why had God allowed this to happen? Couldn't He have stopped it?

Feeling empty and alone, I wept as I begged God to heal my broken heart and body. And that's when the story of my healing began. That's when I felt the inner nudging that can only be explained as God's tender and loving invitation for me to let Him woo my heart.

"Will you get up? Will you trust me?" the Lord asked. "Will you take my hand and dance with me?"

"I don't know how," I cried.

That is when I heard Him say, "Put your feet on top of mine and watch what I can do!"

Lacking the physical strength to get up, I knew God was calling me to a dance of a different kind—the kind that would have Him leading my soul.

Friend, I understand what it's like to be sideswiped and knocked off your feet by hard and unexpected circumstances. I know you do too. Those seasons that leave your heart so shattered, so deeply wounded, that you wonder how or if you will even make it through another day. The barrage of questions that pelt your mind only leaves you feeling more and more confused.

Why is this happening?

Has God forgotten me?

Does God even care?

You look around, and it seems like God is blessing everyone but you. You tell yourself He has passed you by and you are only worthy of His "leftover" love.

It's easy to trust God when things are going well. It's a whole other story when you're in the midst of unspeakable heartache and God seems silent. No matter how hard you try, you can't hear His voice or feel His hand at work.

Having lost all sense of hope, you stare at the wreckage of your life and wonder what you could have done that was so bad it caused God to turn His back on you. All you ever wanted was to love and serve Him with all your heart.

This book is a story of God's ability to take our broken dreams, broken hearts, and broken lives and make something beautiful of them, no matter our story. Throughout its pages, I draw on my professional experience as a trauma therapist and share practical tools that helped me in my own pain-to-promise journey toward healing. More importantly, I offer up my own story so I can be that person for you who says, "I too have felt the way you feel."

Dear friend, how I wish I were sitting there next to you. I'd wrap my arms around you and say, "Me too. I get it! I've felt the sting of pain so great that I wondered how or if I'd find the strength to go on." I want to offer this book as my personal word of encouragement. I want to be that friend beside you who cheers you on.

Just like me, you can and will learn to dance again. I know you don't know how. I know it seems impossible. But I'm asking you to link your arm through mine.

Together, let's take hold of Jesus's hand as we accept His invitation to dance with Him. His feet are big enough for both of us. We can put our feet on His as He promises that He won't let either one of us go.

Remember, while weeping may last for a night, joy comes in the morning (Ps. 30:5).

Who This Book Is for and How to Use It

Loosely inspired by the motif "A time to . . ." in Ecclesiastes 3:1–4, *Healing from Life's Deepest Hurts* serves as a beautiful road map guiding readers through different seasons that lead to healing. I've shared what I personally learned from God in my own journey so that those things can help you too. Each chapter represents a different phase in the process. And while the chapters unfold in a particular order, know that in reality, seasons of healing can come in any order and can even overlap. See these chapters not as a prescription for how and when healing should occur but rather as a picture of what healing looked like in one woman's life—a picture that may prompt some ideas of what healing could look like in your life too.

This book can be used by anyone, whatever challenges they're facing, but it's designed to be especially useful for those who have endured significant loss and pain and who feel emotionally stuck and desire to move forward in their lives. This book is a reminder that no matter how tough things get, healing is always possible.

In each chapter I mix real stories with important teachings from the Bible to offer comfort and direction. Following each chapter, there's a chance to take a break, reflect, and talk with God through prayer. The Tools for Growth and Healing in the back provide practical strategies to help you take steps toward healing. You can find additional tools and resources to complement the chapters in this book by going to HealingFromLifesDeepestHurtsBook.com /Resources or KimberlyHaar.com/Resources. It's important to note that while these tools are valuable, they are not a substitute for professional therapy, medication, or mental health interventions.

Healing from Life's Deepest Hurts sheds light on the profound truth that you have the power to shape your own path with purpose as you navigate life's joys and sorrows. Whatever direction you choose to take and however you decide to move forward, I encourage you to embrace God's love and courageously step into a dance of trust with Him. Join me in this beautiful rhythm, where each step is infused with hope and every movement resonates with the promise of a brighter tomorrow.

1

A TIME TO BE BORN

Rediscovering Your Childlike Faith

Life is the most wonderful fairy tale of all.

Hans Christian Andersen

You saw me before I was born.
  Every day of my life was recorded in your book.
Every moment was laid out
  before a single day had passed.

Psalm 139:16 nlt

The sound of the hospital privacy curtain being abruptly pulled to the side jolted me from my thoughts of the morning. An emergency room nurse slowly approached my bed. Purple latex gloves snapped tightly around her wrists as she prepared to draw a blood sample from my exposed upper right arm. My head throbbed. She tried to distract me with feeble attempts at small talk. Despite her best efforts, nothing numbed the pain. No longer fueled by the adrenaline surge of the last few hours, exhaustion swept over me.

"Where is our daughter? We want to see our daughter!"

I recognized the panicky voices of my parents racing down the hallway toward me.

Unprepared for what they saw, they quickly tried to hide their shock. The look on their faces said it all. I knew that this was bad.

My mother's lip quivered as she bravely attempted a reassuring smile. The tears pooling in her eyes told a different story.

"Are you okay?" she asked, cautiously placing her delicate hand on my bruised and swollen face. Her eyes desperately searched mine for reassurance.

The sound of her voice and those three simple words were all the permission I needed. The floodgates that had held back the tide of emotions finally began to break.

"I don't understand. How could this happen?" I cried. Sobs racked my tired, aching body. My mom stepped toward me and gently pulled me into the cradle of her embrace. One by one, hot tears silently forged their way down my face.

I finally worked up the courage to pick up the little hand mirror from the hospital tray in front of me. To my horror, the hollow eyes gazing back at me belonged to a woman I no longer recognized. Framed by black and blue bruises, my right eye was completely swollen shut. My once soft, brunette hair was now matted with dried blood and stuck to the side of my face.

"Shhh . . . close your eyes and rest," my mother whispered. "I'm here, and I promise it's going to be okay." In that moment, I allowed myself to close my eyes and be held. I listened as my mother's voice reminded me it was all over now and I was finally safe.

The next several hours were a scurry of commotion as one detective after another came in and out of my hospital room. They all seemed to ask the same questions. They wanted to know exactly what I remembered. Over and over again, I had to relive the details of that morning.

One hour turned to two . . . then three. From a chair in the corner of the room, my mom noticed the faraway look in my eyes. She sensed my growing despondency and knew she needed to intervene.

Springing into action, she slipped past the detectives and stepped to my side protectively. Her fingers brushed the hair resting behind my ears, and she whispered something only I could hear. Though my thoughts drifted in and out, making it hard to concentrate, I somehow made out every word she was saying.

"Kim, why don't you sing something?" she asked. Her gaze locked with mine.

While this may seem like an odd request for a mother to make at a time like this, I didn't question what she was saying. Music had always been a big part of my life, having grown up singing in church choirs and listening to praise and worship music. My mom knew that if anything could keep me focused and calm, this would. She feared I might go into shock at any moment.

So, with my mother standing beside me, her hand tightly holding mine, I quietly began to hum. My mind wandered back to the music I had heard just a few days earlier when I attended the wedding of one of my closest friends. On that day, none of this would have seemed possible. On that day, I was filled with joy. On that day, I had danced.

Follow the Leader

Dancing has never been my forte, and I've always been keenly aware of my lack of rhythm. The mere thought of someone witnessing my uncoordinated moves sends me into a cold sweat, and my insecurities take over. In the months leading up to my friend's wedding, I found myself spending countless hours watching tutorials on how to improve my skills. Some well-meaning friends even offered to teach me their moves, but eventually I had to accept the fact that rhythm doesn't come naturally to me. With resignation, I decided to jokingly threaten my friends, warning them not to even walk in my direction when the time came to dance at the reception.

Since I knew some of my friends would think it was funny to get me on the dance floor, there was no way I was going to trust any of them to follow my wishes. So, as a last resort, I searched online for some rules about dancing with a partner. What surprised me was that the first rule wasn't about skill at all—it was about trust. The key to smooth dancing, it said, is having one person lead while the other follows. The leader goes forward, and the follower goes backward.

This made me think of *Dancing with the Stars*, a show I love to watch, where professional dancers teach celebrities to dance in just a few weeks. The celebrities learn how to glide gracefully backward across the floor as the professionals move forward, leading them in the routine they have planned as a team. While it appears effortless, we don't see adjustments being made behind the scenes, even during the competition. We also don't see how each person focuses on their individual role moving backward or forward.

Isn't that just how it is in our relationship with God? More than anything, we desire to trust Him to lead but then get uncomfortable when we can't see where He is taking us. When we feel our back is up against the wall, we soon get out of step and try to take over the lead by going in the direction that feels right to us. Here is what we need to remember: If we keep our eyes on God and allow ourselves to *fully* trust Him, what feels unnatural, scary, or even backward will take us in the right direction. It takes continual practice and intentionality on our part to learn how to take our place as a follower.

> Our heavenly Father loves us so much and desires that we delight in Him and trust Him to catch us when we begin to fall or lose our way.

I stated that I've never been comfortable dancing, but that's not entirely true. There was a time when I danced with joy and abandon. My very first dance partner was larger than life. This man was none other than my grandpa, and the old farmhouse where he and my grandmother lived often turned into our dance floor.

"Hold on tight!" he'd whisper as I placed my tiny feet on top of his, trying not to fall off as his feet moved underneath mine. His eyes twinkled, and his face broke into a grin that deepened the creases around his eyes and forehead. I was his princess and he was my prince, and there was no question that I would follow him anywhere! His rough hands, calloused from years of hard work, engulfed my smaller, delicate ones, and off we went, twirling in circles to the sound of polka music from the old record player in the corner of the room.

What a tremendous earthly example of how God desires us, His children, to trust Him. He wants us to hold on tight and let Him lead us in whatever direction He chooses. Our heavenly Father loves us so much and desires that we delight in Him and trust Him to catch us when we begin to fall or lose our way. Those are the times we must guard against trying to regain control. Those are the times God says, "I know it's scary, but will you trust Me to take the lead?"

When Religion and Rules Get in the Way

I would giggle with delight as Grandpa and I clumsily moved from room to room, his warm voice humming along with the music. Shooting me a mischievous smile, he would dance me into the kitchen where Grandma sat at their small table. This was the same table and chairs I had so often seen my grandparents kneel beside as they bowed their heads in prayer each morning.

Grandma wasn't amused when she glanced up from what she was reading. She pulled her old-fashioned glasses down to the tip of her nose and shot Grandpa "the look" that spoke louder than words and communicated her disapproval. It didn't matter to Grandpa though. He just kept leading me in the dance.

The old farmhouse where my grandparents lived was always one of my favorite places to visit since my family lived several hours away. My grandparents came from Ukraine and settled in a small Canadian town where most people were Mennonites who followed strict religious rules.

In this community, the unspoken rule was that if something was fun, it must therefore be sinful. As someone who took her salvation very seriously and feared crossing the line and incurring God's wrath, my grandmother worked hard at following the so-called "rules."

For instance, watching television was entirely out of the question (until years later when my grandparents got a TV to watch church and the news). Playing cards was considered an abomination. (I remember being told that if I played Solitaire, I was "playing with the devil.") Dyeing your hair was out of the question since this was seen as worldly, and wearing makeup or putting holes in your ears (let alone any other part of your body) was forbidden since this was "defiling the temple." Lastly, above all else, you definitely, *definitely* weren't allowed to dance. (Because you never knew when dancing would lead to other "worldly pleasures.")

Rules, rules, and more rules!

Looking back, I wonder if my grandmother ever truly experienced the joy of seeing God as a heavenly Father who loved and cherished her. Instead, her perception painted Him as a stern figure, someone she dared not displease for fear He might turn His back on her. I guess you could say I inherited the tendency to care too much about what others think, the fear of judgment, and an ingrained need to follow the rules. From a young age, I concluded that there was a right way and a wrong way to do things, leaving little room for anything in between.

> One of God's deepest desires is for us, as His daughters, to approach Him as our heavenly "Daddy."

Carrying the weight of the expectation that I needed to do everything just right fueled my insatiable need to maintain control in every situation. Like my grandma, my desire to please others and do what was deemed "right" was driven by the belief that failing to meet expectations would result in disappointment from those around me and, even more daunting, from God Himself. Little did I know that those beliefs would weave themselves into the very fabric of my life, becoming an imprint I would eventually need to confront. But in those moments with my grandpa, I found contentment in the simple joys of sashaying and twirling and curtsying and dreaming, embracing my childlike innocence.

Have you ever wondered, like I have, if God is disappointed in you? When you fall short of your perception of the "right thing," have you found yourself running *away from* God in shame instead of running *to* Him and seeking His grace? Do you see God as a distant father or strict taskmaster just waiting for an opportunity to punish you?

Here's the truth: One of God's deepest desires is for us, as His daughters, to approach Him as our heavenly "Daddy." He longs for us to crawl onto His lap where He can lavish us with His boundless love. Listen closely—can you hear His tender call wooing you to come closer? Can you hear Him calling out your name? He stands ready and waiting, arms open wide to welcome you with love. He is eager to embrace you!

Cinderella Dreams and "Cake Pan" Faith

In the summer of 1973, my parents decided to relocate our family from Canada to Oklahoma, where at the time we knew no one. With our meager belongings packed tightly into a small U-Haul trailer, my two siblings and I squished into the back seat of our green Oldsmobile. Moving a thousand miles away from everything and everyone familiar to us marked the beginning of a new adventure.

Even though I missed the family we had left behind, I quickly adapted to my new surroundings. I made new friends and indulged in harmless childhood mischief. Hour upon hour, I played with my Ken and Barbie dolls, dreaming and planning for the fairy-tale life I knew I would one day lead.

In addition to playing Barbies and games with friends, I was always intrigued hearing about the stories in the Bible. My innocent faith allowed me to believe that anything God said was unquestionably true. It was as simple as that.

One evening, when I was eight years old, my parents left my siblings and me with a babysitter. Out of nowhere, a storm arose, and the sky turned an ominous gray. My heart skipped a beat as I hurried to the living room window. I strained to see through the thick blanket of rain that pelted the ground. I watched with trepidation as the water in the creek that backed right up to our house continued to rise. As the water rose higher and higher, so did my fear.

Under my breath, I quietly began to plead with God, asking Him to watch over my house and keep all of us safe. I reminded

Him of a story in the Bible I had heard just a few nights earlier. It was about a man named Noah who built an ark, and God saved him and his family from a devastating flood. I read how God placed a rainbow in the sky as His promise to never flood the whole earth again.

Summoning all the eight-year-old boldness I could muster, I adamantly reminded God of this promise and how the Bible said God could not break His promises. Over and over, I told God I knew I could trust Him. The rising creek water never reached my home that night, nor in all the years we continued to live there.

Eventually my fear of flooding subsided, but other fears called out my name. Nighttime seemed to be the worst. Whenever I heard an unfamiliar noise, my imagination ran wild. I'd be sure an intruder was trying to get into our house. When I became scared, I'd stop whatever I was doing and drop to my knees and pray. With a fervent plea, I'd ask God to please put a cake pan of protection over my home.

Let me elaborate. You see, I'd often watched my mother put a freshly baked cake on a pedestal plate with a clear glass cover over it. It not only preserved the cake's freshness but also kept it safely out of reach from all of us children. I figured if Mom could do this, I could certainly ask God to do the same thing. I envisioned God putting a transparent force field over our home—just like that glass cover over Mom's cake—that would keep all intruders away. I prayed that if an intruder even *thought* about breaking into our home, this force field would stop them and make it impossible for them to come anywhere near my family.

My list of worries and concerns may have seemed childish and unimportant to many people, but they were significant to me and to God. God saw my childlike faith and knew I trusted Him to honor His promise to protect me.

Too often, we dismiss the things that concern us as trivial and convince ourselves they don't matter to God. Oh, sweet friend, let me assure you that when it comes to prayer, there is no request too big or too small. Just as God heeded my earnest prayer for a cake pan of protection at the tender age of eight, He cares deeply about the things that matter to you. He not only welcomes you to pour out your desires to Him but also takes delight in them. As parents, nothing brings us greater joy than fulfilling the heartfelt wishes of our children. How much more does our heavenly Father delight in us, His beloved children, when we approach Him with our hopes and dreams?

So I ask you, What are the secret desires of your heart? You know, the ones you're embarrassed or hesitant to tell anyone else about because they seem insignificant or too far out of reach. Take a moment and write them down. Psalm 139 says God already knows our thoughts from afar. That means there's nothing you can think about that God doesn't already know. The beautiful part is that He's eager and waiting for you to come to Him and ask!

Becoming Like Little Children

Maintaining a childlike faith in difficult times can be challenging. After enduring hardships, it's easy to adopt a jaded attitude. However, having a childlike faith is vital during times of tragedy and pain because it allows us to approach life with trust and openness, much like how a child views the world. Children inherently believe in the goodness of others and the possibility of miracles, even when facing adversity. This type of faith can offer comfort and hope, reminding us that despite the pain we endure, there is still beauty and wonder to be found in the world.

The Bible records several instances where Jesus spoke of His desire for adults to become like little children. In Matthew 18:2–4 we read, "He called a little child to him, and placed the child among them. And he said: 'Truly I tell you, unless you change and become like little children, you will never enter the kingdom of heaven. Therefore, whoever takes the lowly position of this child is the greatest in the kingdom of heaven.'" The Greek word used here for "child" is *paidion*, which refers to the youngest and most helpless child.[1] Jesus was saying He wants us to depend on Him just as an infant depends on a caregiver for its every need.

We see in Mark 10:13–16 that Jesus even became angry when the disciples stood in the way of those trying to bring children to Him so He could bless them. It reads:

> And they were bringing children to him that he might touch them, and the disciples rebuked them. But when Jesus saw it, he was indignant and said to them, "Let the children come to me; do not hinder them, for to such belongs the kingdom of God. Truly, I say to you, whoever does not receive the kingdom of God like a child shall not enter it." And he took them in his arms and blessed them, laying his hands on them. (ESV)

I wonder what the disciples thought when they heard this. Why would Jesus say that adults needed to change and become more like little children? Let's consider just a few characteristics of children that will help us better understand His words.

In a healthy relationship, children have absolute confidence in their parents. They believe without hesitation in their love and reliability. Similarly, God desires that we place our trust in Him and understand His boundless love and steadfastness toward us. God desires for us to recognize His limitless power and sovereignty over all things in the same way children view their parents as being able to do anything. Embracing this childlike trust, even in the face of uncertainty, allows us to rely on God's promises with unwavering confidence, knowing that His plans for us are rooted in love and wisdom beyond our understanding.

Children have an innate ability to trust their parents to care for their every need. They know they'll have food, a warm bed to sleep in, loving arms to hold them, and toys to play with, so they can just focus on being kids and having fun. Such innocent trust becomes especially vital when we're facing tragedy or loss. Just like children trust their parents to provide for them, God wants us to trust Him to take care of us, even in our darkest moments. This idea connects with what Jesus says in Matthew 6:25–26, where He reminds us not to stress about basic needs like food and clothes, because just as God takes care of the birds, He'll surely take care of us too.

As adults, we often pride ourselves on being independent, but sometimes that pride stops us from asking for help when we need it. Learning from children means admitting we can't do everything on our own and turning to God for help, saying, "God, I need You in this." It's about recognizing our reliance on Him, especially during tough times, and trusting Him to provide what we need.

Children are naturally curious, carefree, and able to live in the moment. They are fully engaged with the present and allow their imaginations to run free, finding joy in the simplest of things. God calls us to embrace this childlike approach, to cherish each day instead of getting bogged down by anxieties about the future. When we face tough seasons, maintaining this childlike faith and tendency to focus on the present can be crucial. It allows us to find beauty and joy amid hardship, trusting that God is with us in every moment.

Children are bold and aren't afraid to ask for what they want or to speak their minds. If your kids are anything like mine, you've probably had times when you held your breath and prayed they would not embarrass you with something they said. I'll never forget the time my daughter's sweet, older first-grade teacher told me how my daughter had been patiently waiting for a turn to talk to her. As she waited, my daughter began to flick and play with the excess skin that hung from the underside of the teacher's upper arm. After a few flicks, my daughter innocently looked up at the teacher and told her that her arm was just like the cow's udder she had seen at the petting zoo the previous day. I'm not sure who was more mortified that day—the teacher or me! As the old saying goes, if you want to know what a child is thinking, just ask them.

Obviously, children aren't too concerned about what others think. That's why if a child wants something, they are quick to ask for it without fear of being reproved. Hebrews 4:16 says we are to have that same kind of confidence and boldness in telling God what we are thinking: "Therefore let us [with privilege] approach the throne of grace [that is, the throne of God's gracious favor] with confidence and without fear, so that we may receive mercy [for our failures] and find [His amazing] grace to help in time of need [an appropriate blessing, coming just at the right moment]" (AMP).

> Our persistence in prayer demonstrates our unwavering belief in God's promises and invites His active intervention in our lives, even amid our challenges.

Having the courage to approach God with childlike boldness is particularly vital during times of struggle and hardship. This childlike faith empowers us to seek refuge in His loving embrace and find the strength and support we need to navigate life's challenges with courage and resilience.

Children are persistent! They don't stop asking until they get what they want. I think of the many times my children constantly reminded me about something I had promised them but had not yet delivered on. Isaiah 43:26 tells us to do that very same thing with God. This verse starts by saying, "Put me in remembrance" (KJV). In other words, "Remind me of what I've said." Reminding God of His promises is also reminding ourselves of His promises and of His faithfulness. In Jeremiah 1:12, we read, "Then the LORD said to me, 'You have seen well, for I am [actively] watching over My word to fulfill it'" (AMP). Our persistence in prayer demonstrates our unwavering belief in God's promises and invites His active intervention in our lives, even amid our challenges.

30

Turn to God with the Faith of a Child

Those early days following my visit to the emergency room were a crucial time in my physical and emotional recovery. Holding on to a childlike faith allowed me to believe that God would somehow get me through these darkest moments, even though I couldn't imagine how.

Stop for a moment and think about a problem or crisis you are currently facing. Are you taking a childlike perspective or a more jaded, adult one? Are you being bold and persistent with what you are asking of God? Do you know what God's perspective of the situation is? To understand what God has promised you, begin by studying the Scriptures. You can then be certain you are praying God's will. Remind God of what He has said, not because He has forgotten but because it reinforces our trust and faith in His unchanging nature. He gave us His Word for guidance. Scripture states that when we pray according to God's will, we can have confidence that He hears us (1 John 5:14).

So, what is childlike faith? It is simply believing there is nothing too difficult for God. It is believing He will do what He says He will do and having confidence in His love for us. More than mere belief, childlike faith is a profound trust in God's capability, a confidence in knowing there is nothing beyond His power.

During infancy we rely on caregivers, but as we grow, we begin to transition toward self-reliance. Similarly, in our faith journey we start off young and immature in our beliefs. As we mature, however, we often find ourselves substituting our plans for God's, relying on our own understanding rather than seeking His guidance. We ask God to bless *our* plans without asking Him if this is what He wants for us. We even convince ourselves that because we want something bad enough, it must mean God wants the same thing. Before long, God's Word and His promises are no longer sufficient for us. We fall into the trap of doubting God, and we begin to question if He knows what He's doing. Slowly but surely, we take matters into our own hands.

When God's plans begin to lead us down a route different from the one we had planned, we are quick to turn into backseat drivers. We tell God which turn on the road He should take, how fast we think He should drive, and when it's time to stop the car and let us out. Country singer Carrie Underwood had it right when she sang, "Jesus, take the wheel!"

> While we might not understand God's plan, it's important not to buy into the devil's lie that God doesn't have one. It just means we don't see the whole picture.

When difficulties arise, it can become easy to forget that God knows the beginning from the end, and He knows the things we don't. His plans for us are so much greater than anything we could ever imagine on our own. While we might not understand God's plan, it's important not to buy into the devil's lie that God doesn't have one. It just means we don't see the whole picture. Jeremiah 29:11 states, "'For I know the plans I have for you,' says the LORD. 'They are plans for good and not for disaster, to give you a future and a hope'" (NLT).

God is our heavenly Father, and He asks us, His children, to have a childlike faith that trusts, totally relies on, and completely depends on Him. God is inviting us to trust His heart even when we can't fully grasp His plans. Won't you join me in saying yes?

PAUSE AND REFLECT

- Think back to the days of your childhood hopes and dreams. What were your conversations with God like? Describe them.
- Reflect on Mark 10:14–15, where Jesus speaks of the importance of having a childlike faith. What does childlike faith mean to you?
- Can you identify times that perceived "rules of religion" have stood in your way of going deeper in your walk with the Lord?
- When children ask questions, they typically aren't afraid to speak their honest thoughts. They have an incredible ability to trust even when they don't understand something. When was the last time you expressed your honest thoughts to the Lord? Emulating the faith of a child, pray and ask God to help you take Him at His word.

PRAYER OF OUR HEART

Father, I ask You to restore to me the joy of my salvation and bring me back to an innocent, childlike faith so I can trust You, knowing how very much You love me. Remind me of the dreams You placed in my heart and lead me to the dreams You have for me. Help me to trust You even in times I don't understand what Your plans are for me. Please help me to realize Your plans are good. Give me the courage and confidence I need to follow Your lead even when things don't make sense to my natural mind. The cry of my heart is to trust You, Jesus! In Your mighty name I pray. Amen.

2

A TIME TO LET GO

The Gift of Goodbye

Some think that holding on makes us strong, but sometimes it's letting go.

HERMAN HESSE

You keep track of all my sorrows.
　　You have collected all my tears in your bottle.
　　You have recorded each one in your book.

PSALM 56:8 NLT

At the tender age of twenty-two, I met the man who would soon become my fiancé, and I fully expected my fairy-tale life to unfold. Just like every relationship, ours had its ups and downs, but I felt no real concern that anything was out of the ordinary. Our wedding day, the year after we met, was the day I had dreamed of my whole life. The weather was beautiful, and many of our friends and family had traveled a long way to share in our celebration.

My form-fitting dress shimmered with pearls and lace, and a sheer fingertip veil gently covered my face. I nervously awaited the moment the doors to the church auditorium would open to announce the bride's entry.

The music got louder, and the wedding march began to play as I gently slipped my hand into the crook of my father's arm. Together, we started the slow march down the center aisle to the altar where my handsome young groom stood. This was the day we would promise before God and others to love, honor, and respect each other for the rest of our lives.

Unfortunately, my story didn't unfold like the "happily ever after" fairy tales. Instead of feeling like the princess from Cinderella, I soon felt more like Humpty Dumpty, shattered and unable to piece myself back together. Within a few years, the cracks in my fairy-tale marriage began to show. I discovered that my husband had been unfaithful, and from that point on, my marriage was a roller coaster of highs and lows. Though his behavior would occasionally improve for a time, his infidelity remained a persistent issue, leading to a cycle of destruction that repeated itself year after year. It's worth noting that while my husband's behavior was damaging, he had never been physically abusive.

On the day we exchanged vows, I had made a solemn promise before God to stand by my husband "for better or worse," and I took those words to heart. I never considered a divorce; in my mind it simply wasn't an option. At the time our problems began, we had two young children, and their presence only reinforced my commitment to weather the storms. Wanting them to grow up with an intact family, I chose to forgive and forgive and forgive again.

A Question of Loyalty

As Christians, we are taught to fight for our marriages and families, and that's exactly what I set out to do. For twenty-three years I clung to my faith, fervently praying for the restoration of my marriage. Despite our efforts to seek guidance from multiple marriage counselors, my husband's pattern of infidelity persisted.

During the later years of my marriage, my relationship to therapy deepened as I embarked on a journey to become a therapist myself. This professional pursuit not only facilitated my personal growth but also deepened my understanding of boundaries and relational dynamics.

One book that had a big impact on me at the time was *Necessary Endings* by Henry Cloud. In it, Cloud writes, "Loyalty is important, one of the most important character traits we can have. But loyal love does not mean infinite and/or misplaced responsibility for another's life, nor does it mean that one forever puts up with mistreatment out of inappropriate loyalty."[1]

I was not the perfect wife by any means. I made more than my fair share of mistakes along the way. However, if there was one thing I could be certain of, it was my unwavering loyalty. Yet, as time went on, it became evident that my husband's consistent disloyalty was unlikely to ever change. With my two youngest children at the tender age of fifteen and my older two at nineteen and twenty-one, I was forced to confront a harsh reality. My husband's behavior had reached a point of no return, and I could no longer ignore the truth or turn a blind eye to it. At a pivotal crossroads, I found myself grappling with a profound choice: Would I continue in an empty marriage? Or would I prioritize loyalty to myself, to my children, and to the boundaries I had painstakingly established?

With much prayer, soul-searching, and counsel from trusted advisers, I faced the most agonizing decision of my life. But after twenty-three years of marriage, the day finally came when I'd had enough. I summoned the courage to initiate divorce proceedings.

Just the thought of meeting with a lawyer brought every feeling of vulnerability and insecurity to the surface. I knew there was no way I would be able to face this alone, so I called and enlisted my dad's company for moral support. We decided we would meet at a local tire shop and drive to the lawyer's office together.

When the day came, I was the first to arrive. I stayed in my car and turned from one radio station to another, trying to drown out the gnawing ache in my heart. Relief washed over me when I heard gravel crunching beneath tire treads as my dad pulled into the parking spot next to mine. Before he could even shut the door to his car, I ran into my dad's arms and buried my face in his shoulder. Tears streamed down my face.

"Dad, promise me I'm not making the wrong decision," I cried, desperate for his reassurance. "Promise me I'm not making a mistake."

I had fought for my marriage so long and so hard that surrendering now felt like I was questioning and giving up on God.

Gently pushing me away from him, my dad lovingly looked down into my upturned face.

"Kim, this doesn't have to be the end," he said. "If your husband decides to change his ways, you can always remarry him at a later time."

My father's look was one of deep sadness as we sat quietly side by side on the drive to the lawyer's office. A single tear slipped down his face.

"Is This a Good Thing?"

Three months passed, my husband had moved out, and the day came for our divorce to be made final.

The day before the proceedings, my lawyer told me, "Tomorrow, all you have to do is meet me at the courthouse. It should be a relatively quick and easy process. Someone will show you into the judge's chambers, swear you in, and shortly after that you will be pronounced divorced." I left his office with my stomach in knots.

My alarm clock rang bright and early. This was the day I had dreaded. Hesitantly, I dialed the number I was so used to calling by now.

"Dad . . .?"

My one-word plea was met with the only response I needed to hear: "I'm here!"

Together, we embarked on the long drive to the courthouse. Tears silently fell as I stared out the passenger window. My throat tightened, making it hard to breathe. Understanding that no words could console me, my dad gave me the gift of silence and honored the space for my private pain.

When we arrived at the courthouse, I made the long walk from where we parked to the front doors of the large, redbrick building. I reached for the handle with trembling palms. I felt like I was about to be judged as a horrible wife.

Why couldn't I get my marriage to survive?

What was wrong with me giving up on a twenty-three-year marriage?

The accusations slung in my direction weren't coming from a prosecuting attorney. They were coming from my own inner judge.

"Follow me," the court clerk said, leading the way to the judge's chambers. Dutifully, I followed. Much to my surprise, instead of a formidable and stoic judge like the ones I had seen on TV, a pleasant, middle-aged woman looked up from her desk and greeted me with a smile.

"Good morning. I see you are getting a divorce today. Is this a good thing?"

A good thing? A good thing?! I mentally screamed at her in anger and disbelief. I wondered how anyone in their right mind could possibly consider any divorce a "good thing." While I knew my decision today was the *right thing* for me to do, this divorce meant my family had been torn apart. Promises had been broken. Dreams had been shattered. My children's parents were no longer together. I was now going to have to navigate beginning a new life alone.

No, Judge, it is not a good thing. It is not a good thing at all. Not for me or anyone else involved.

Return to Sender—Damaged Goods!

In a little less than thirty minutes, the judge's gavel came down with a thud, marking the official end of my marriage. It was done. With a solemn nod from the court clerk, I gathered my belongings and followed him to the adjacent hallway where my dad stood waiting. He had been there to walk me down the wedding aisle twenty-three years earlier. This time he was waiting to take me back home.

In that precise moment, a wave of embarrassment and humiliation washed over me from head to toe. Vulnerable and exposed, I became a target for the devil's echoing accusations that I had fallen short and failed. I felt like a return package to a department store, rejected and unwanted. The stamp emblazoned on my heart now read "Damaged Goods!"

Isn't that just like the devil, hitting us when we're down? John 10:10 tells us that the devil "comes only to steal and kill and destroy." He cunningly watches for our weak, vulnerable moments when he can roar his words of accusation at us. These lies take root in our hearts and minds, especially in times of heartache, loss, and disappointment. It then becomes easy to believe these lies are true, especially when circumstances seemingly provide further evidence against us.

In 1 Peter 5:8, the apostle Peter warns us, "Stay alert! Watch out for your great enemy, the devil. He prowls around like a roaring lion, looking for someone to devour" (NLT). The words "enemy," "prowl," "roaring," and "devour" are not passive, nor are they for the weak at heart. Merriam-Webster defines the verb *devour* as "to destroy all trace of."[2] When something is devoured, it is depleted, drained, exhausted, annihilated, demolished, devastated, or done in. And the morning I walked out of that courtroom, that was exactly how I felt.

I know I'm not the only one. What are the times in your own life when you also have felt under attack by the devil? What words of accusation have repeatedly echoed in your ears and knocked you off your feet without warning? What accusing lies of the devil have shaken you to your core?

Exposing the Lie of Shame

Navigating the relentless attacks of the devil can be challenging, especially when it comes to the battleground of our self-worth. The devil is on a mission to devastate and destroy all traces of us! One of the ways he does this is by getting us to believe his accusing words of shame.

In my work as a therapist, I often emphasize the crucial distinction between guilt and shame. Guilt addresses our behavior; its primary purpose is to convict and motivate us to positive change. Shame unfairly condemns us as a person, and its purpose is to accuse and point fingers at us.

Guilt says, "I failed at something." Shame maliciously whispers, "I am a failure."

Guilt admits, "I made a mistake." Shame harshly declares, "I am a mistake."

Guilt says, "I did something unloving." Shame says, "I am unlovable."

One day, in my office, I began explaining the difference between guilt and shame to a client. I started writing the word "shame" on the large whiteboard mounted in the middle of my wall. I had demonstrated this example hundreds of times before. This time, however, something stopped me in my tracks.

> The devil wants to hide his taunting thoughts so only we can hear. That's because he knows that if he can get us to believe his lies, he will have us exactly where he wants us.

As I began to write, I paused when I realized the first two letters of "shame" are S-H, which sounds like "Shh!" That's what we say when we want to keep something hidden or don't want our words to be heard by others. "Shh! Don't tell anybody I told you this!" "Shh! Keep this a secret!"

It dawned on me how that is the exact same thing the devil whispers to us. He lies to us and tries to convince us that what he says is true. His secret accusations often turn into what is known as negative internal self-talk, and it can sound something like this:

What will people think of you now?

You're such a loser!

Nobody will like you!

It's all your fault!

Does any of this sound familiar? Recognizing these whispers for what they are—lies—is the first step to breaking free from their grip. The devil wants to hide his taunting thoughts so only we can hear. That's because he knows that if he can get us to believe his lies, he will have us exactly where he wants us.

Fighting Back Against the Author of Lies

As I continued to spell out the word "shame" on my whiteboard, I paused once more when I came to the fourth letter: S-H-A-M. The letters staring back at me now spelled *sham*. Sham describes something that is false or not genuine, and related words include "fake," "false," "unauthentic," "fabricated," "deceptive," "misleading," "counterfeit," and "bluff."[3] In other words, a sham is a lie.

The devil's specialty is knowing just when and how to hit below the belt. In Revelation 12:10, he is called "the accuser." More often than not, the negative beliefs he whispers in our ears get repeated and reinforced when life experiences deeply wound us. First Peter 5:8 describes the devil as roaming around *like a roaring lion.* He wants us to believe he is the king of the jungle when in reality he's just a fake.

In the iconic 1939 film *The Wizard of Oz*, Dorothy and her friends return to Oz with the Wicked Witch of the West's broomstick, hoping to claim their promised rewards. However, when they present the broomstick to the Wizard, he hesitates and sends them away, promising to fulfill their wishes the next day. Frustrated by the delay, Dorothy and her companions confront the Wizard. That's when Toto pulls back a curtain to reveal a small man orchestrating elaborate illusions to appear more powerful than he is. As the truth comes to light, the Wizard speaks into the microphone and says, "Pay no attention to the man behind the curtain!"[4] This is the moment his true nature is exposed for Dorothy and her friends.

> We can only counterattack the devil and his lies by knowing and speaking what the Word of God says.

That's a good analogy for how the devil works. Like the Wizard hiding behind the curtain, the devil uses his metaphorical loudspeaker to convince us of his lies and make himself seem bigger than he is. Thank God we know he's a fraud! We can only counterattack the devil and his lies by knowing and speaking what the Word of God says. Just like Toto exposed the Wizard, the truth of God's Word dismantles the devil's deceit.

- When the devil says, "You're worthless!" God's Word says, "You were bought with a price!"

    God bought you with a high price. So you must honor God with your body. (1 Cor. 6:20 NLT)

- When the devil says, "You were a mistake!" God's Word says, "I planned you before you were born!"

    Before I shaped you in the womb, I knew all about you. Before you saw the light of day, I had holy plans for you. (Jer. 1:5 MSG)

- When the devil says, "You're all alone!" God's Word says, "I will never leave you or forsake you!"

    Be strong and courageous. Do not be afraid or terrified because of them, for the LORD your God goes with you; he will never leave you nor forsake you. (Deut. 31:6)

- When the devil says, "You can't be forgiven!" God's Word says, "He is faithful and just to forgive and cleanse us."

    If we confess our sins, he is faithful and just and will forgive us our sins and purify us from all unrighteousness. (1 John 1:9)

- The devil is not only full of lies, he is the father of lies!

    [The devil] was a murderer from the beginning. He has always hated the truth, because there is no truth in him. When he lies, it is consistent with his character; for he is a liar and the father of lies. (John 8:44 NLT)

The day I walked out of that courthouse, shame enveloped me like a thick, wet, suffocating blanket. It weighed me down and sucked the air out of my lungs until I felt I could no longer breathe. The accusations flung by the devil echoed in my ears and sounded something like this:

You're such a failure!
You are a humiliation to your family!
Your husband didn't want you!
God can't use you now!
You are such an impostor as a marriage and family therapist!
You couldn't even save your own marriage!
You will be such a laughingstock!

And the list went on and on.

When Satan Attacks Your Self-Worth

One way the devil tightens his grip on us is by sucking us into the comparison trap. We begin to measure our value against others and what we see in the highlight reels of social media. We catch glimpses of other people's lives without seeing the whole picture of what goes on behind closed doors, and we convince ourselves that we somehow fall short, are not as good, or for whatever reason must not be worth loving.

In stories about proms and dances, teenage girls are sometimes depicted as awkwardly sitting on the sidelines as "wallflowers." A girl in this situation is the one no one has asked to dance. She feels unwanted, humiliated, and invisible. Life is full of moments of not being chosen. Perhaps you've experienced such a moment yourself. It's in times like these that messages regarding our value are written on our hearts.

Our self-worth comes under attack when we either hear from others or tell ourselves messages that we aren't [fill in the blank] enough:

"You aren't smart enough!"
"You aren't pretty enough!"
"You aren't good enough!"
"You aren't skinny enough!"
"You aren't skilled enough!"
"You aren't funny enough!"
(You get the idea.)

Stop! Comparing yourself to others will only steal your joy. It makes you want what others have (or what you think they have) and plants seeds of discontent in your mind. You begin to believe the lie that God has favorites and you aren't one of them. You tell yourself that all you are worthy of is God's "leftover" love. Let me reassure you that there is no such thing. God's Word says He is "rich in love" (Ps. 145:8).

For months following my divorce, I compared myself to every married woman I saw. I wondered what I had done that was so bad it cost me my husband's love. I echoed the devil's lies and told myself, "I must not have been enough." I concluded something about me must have made me unworthy of love. Shame seemed to follow me everywhere. I saw myself in a negative light and believed the lie that I was now branded with a scarlet letter *D*.

Divorced.
Disqualified.
Devalued.
Defective.
Disappointment.

Tour of Grief: Past, Present, and Future

Recognizing the need to heal, I committed to facing the pain, which involved acknowledging the unspoken grief I carried. While I had been the one who initiated the divorce, there were moments when my pain felt unbearable. Unbeknownst to me, I had been grieving the death of my marriage long before I ever filed for divorce. I had been grieving the past, present, and future.

I grieved over the lost "happily ever after" dreams of my childhood. I mourned the unmet expectations of what I thought my marriage *could* and *should* have been. And I grieved the realization that my marriage was never going to be any of those things.

Years later, I was watching television when a news story caught my attention. It was about a female orca whale named J35 who had a calf that survived only hours after birth. For more than two weeks the world watched as this mother whale carried her dead calf—over six feet long and weighing hundreds of pounds—on her back as she swam for more than a thousand miles off the Pacific Northwest coast. It was heartbreaking to witness. Each time the calf slipped off her back, the mother whale dove to retrieve it and prevent it from sinking. The news referred to this as an "unprecedented period of mourning" that lasted longer than scientists had ever seen before. Even though the calf's body had begun to decompose, this mother whale was unwilling to let go, despite the risk to her own health.

After seventeen days, J35 finally said goodbye and allowed her dead calf to slide from her back and sink to the ocean floor. The news media labeled her journey as a "tour of grief."[5]

Sitting on the couch and watching this story unfold, I was reminded that I, too, understood what a tour of grief felt like. I had grieved and held on to a marriage that had begun to decompose years earlier. The time had finally come for me to let it go.

A Time to Let Go

I knew that starting over was not going to be easy. On the one hand, I was ready for a fresh start. On the other hand, I still held on to a spark of hope that my marriage could one day be restored.

At the time of my divorce, I decided I would remain single and not date anyone for the next four years. My two youngest children were still in high school, and it was important to me that they not feel forgotten or replaced. I didn't want them to feel like they had to compete with anyone else for my attention.

I had a candid conversation with my ex-husband. I told him if during this four-year period he made substantial changes—including a renewed commitment to God, stability in his employment, and a genuine accountability for his past infidelities with evidence of changed behavior—I might someday be willing to revisit the idea of a possible reconciliation. I made it unequivocally clear that my foremost responsibility was safeguarding our children. They deserved a stable and secure environment. I vowed to shield them from the emotional roller coaster we had all endured and were just beginning to recover from.

> Sometimes we hold on because we've held on for so long that we forget why we were holding on in the first place.

As the four-year mark approached and our youngest children entered college, I reflected on the journey. While there had been some minor shifts in my ex-husband's behavior, they fell short of the transformation I had hoped for. It was a sobering realization that despite my best efforts, I couldn't control the outcome of our marriage—a dream that had slowly faded with time. Facing this reality, I came to terms with the impact of someone else's decisions and committed to charting a fresh path forward, one built on self-respect and inner worth.

Sometimes we hold on to things for the wrong reasons. We hold on tightly because we're afraid to let go. We hold on out of guilt or to avoid the judgment of others. And sometimes we hold on because we've held on for so long that we forget why we were holding on in the first place. That's where I found myself as I considered whether I again needed to let go of my marriage and any possibility of reconciliation—but completely this time.

One evening I happened to be listening to a sermon on YouTube by a well-known pastor and heard him say, "You've got to know when people's part in your story is over so that you don't keep trying to raise the dead." He challenged me to let go of the past rather than staying stuck there. Instead of continuing to try and handle the situation myself, he challenged me to take my hands off it and let God do a new thing. Again and again I heard him say, "Let it go!"[6]

That's when I knew that after twenty-three years of holding on to a marriage that had died a long time before, it was finally time for me to let it go.

As you read this, I want to encourage you to do some soul-searching of your own. Are there areas in your life you've been holding on to that, deep down, you know the Lord is asking you to let go of? This might resonate with you if you've been tightly gripping something, fearing it might slip away. Perhaps it's not a spouse but an unfulfilled dream for your future, a friendship that has reached its end, or a job you've outgrown.

Are you ready to trust God and lay those things at His feet? Can you say, "Not my will, but yours be done"? It's about surrendering your plan to His. As Isaiah 43:18–19 says, "Forget the former things; do not dwell on the past. See, I am doing a new thing!"

This chapter is not advocating for divorce. God can and does heal broken marriages that have been deeply wounded, but God has also given humankind free will and the ability to think for ourselves. God will not impose His will on anyone. There are biblical reasons for divorce. If you find yourself struggling in your relationships and are unsure what to do, seek out a wise Christian counselor or pastor who can partner with you, understand your situation, and offer sound, biblical counsel.

—————————— **PAUSE AND REFLECT** ——————————

- After reading this chapter, describe a time the devil attacked you with his lies. Have you ever told yourself that you're unwanted, unlovable, disqualified, defective, unworthy, not good enough, or that something is wrong with you? If so, the devil has you right where he wants you.
- The devil hates the truth and is incapable of telling it. Take out a sheet of paper and make two columns on it. In the left column, list any lie or negative belief you've allowed yourself to believe. Then, in the right column, list what the Word of God says about you and this situation. (See "The Power of Self-Talk" in the Tools for Growth and Healing.)
- Meditate on Psalm 119:105: "Your word is a lamp for my feet, a light on my path." Darkness cannot stay where there is light.

—————————— **PRAYER OF OUR HEART** ——————————

Father, I ask You to give me the strength and confidence to know when I am hearing Your voice. Your Word says that Your sheep know Your voice and don't follow a stranger's voice. Help me discern the enemy's lies and guard my heart and mind against them. Please help me recognize the times when You are asking me to stay and the times when You are telling me to let go. Help me let go of past hurts and pain and become willing to move forward with Your forgiveness. In Jesus's name I pray. Amen.

3

A TIME TO LAUGH

Joy in the Midst of Sorrow

Laughter is a holy thing. It is as sacred as music.

ANNE LAMOTT

A merry heart does good, like medicine,
But a broken spirit dries the bones.

PROVERBS 17:22 NKJV

Soon after I filed for divorce in 2013, I decided it might be therapeutic for me to try this thing called blogging that everyone seemed to be talking about. Basically, it looked like writing in a diary, except it was done on the computer instead of in a notebook. It looked like fun, so I thought, "Why not?" and bravely decided to give it a try.

My interest was piqued when I saw the pretty backgrounds and fonts I could choose from to complement my writing. As I began to type, I wrote that this would be my journey toward finding my "true self" as I healed from the effects of going through a divorce.

My fingers began to fly over the computer keyboard. Sparing no details, I poured my raw, uncensored emotions onto the written page. (Did I mention it was uncensored?) Using my real name, real vocation, and a real picture of myself, I wrote candidly about everything I felt. I held nothing back and left *absolutely nothing* to the imagination.

A few nights later a close friend came over to visit. I couldn't wait to tell her about my "private" blog and how it was proving to be very therapeutic for me.

"You won't believe how much fun this is!" I began to share excitedly. "I'm the only one who can see this, but maybe someday, if I ever get brave enough, I just might consider sharing it with others."

My friend asked the name of my blog, so I told her. I watched as she typed something into her phone. It took only a few minutes before she looked up at me with an amused smirk.

"Kim, come over here and see what I found!" She giggled.

To my absolute horror and dismay, there on her very public iPhone screen was my very private blog for all the world to see. My heart raced, and I felt like I was going to throw up. I panicked, begging her to quickly help me delete my words that had vulnerably expressed the uncensored thoughts of my heart. No one could ever see this! I didn't care if I lost everything I had so carefully written—I just wanted every last bit of it gone.

Looking back now, it must have seemed like an episode of *I Love Lucy* where Ethel tries to save Lucy from one of her many harebrained ideas. The more we tried unsuccessfully to delete the blog, the funnier my friend thought it was. The words "error message" kept appearing on my computer screen, saying I didn't have permission to delete anything. The error message said my blog was linked to my company email. (I didn't even know what "linked" meant!) To make matters worse, my computer kept telling me if I wanted to make changes, I would need to contact my company's IT department and get special permission to access the account.

How could this get any worse?

Humiliation and sheer panic coursed through my body as I pictured my entire agency, the board of directors, and all my therapy clients reading the highly personal things I had written that were intended for my eyes only.

That night I barely slept. As I lay awake worrying, I decided that on the way to work the next day, I would stop at the nearby bakery, pick up some donuts, and proceed to bribe the company's IT department to help me delete my "true confessions."

The next morning as I walked into the IT office, my heart was pounding so loud I was sure it might jump out of my chest. "Ahem!" I cleared my throat to gain the attention of the woman working there. Sheepishly, I squeaked out my request for her to come help me with something.

Once my office door was securely latched behind us, I knew the time had come for me to confess this awful thing I had done and plead for mercy.

"Please, *please* promise you won't tell anyone. I think I've done something really foolish." My eyes brimmed with tears as I began to tell her of the predicament I had gotten myself into. I apologized profusely. "I'm so embarrassed! It wasn't my intent to do anything to cause embarrassment to our agency. If you help me just this once, I promise I'll never let anything like this ever happen again."

The woman from IT attempted (unsuccessfully, I must add) to hold back her chuckle as she began to type her magic. I nervously hovered over her shoulder and watched with desperate anticipation. It took just a few mouse clicks and taps until the blog I had created suddenly appeared on the screen. I held my breath and felt my panic and urgency rising. I was sure that millions of people would have read this by now.

After what seemed like an eternity, the woman turned toward me and gave a comforting smile. "I'm not sure what you saw," she said, "but there is nothing here that links this to our company information."

Releasing my breath, I didn't know whether to laugh or cry. I had confessed my blunder for nothing. With an apple fritter bribe in hand and a smile on her face, the woman got up from my chair and headed back toward her office. Under my breath, I prayed she would keep my secret safe, but I could hear her laughter echoing from down the hall.

When my heart finally quit racing, I sighed with relief, at last seeing the humor of the previous twenty-four hours. What had begun as a private journey of finding myself had quickly turned into what I believed was the whole world wide web finding me as well. I decided that before I ever thought about sharing my private feelings or thoughts again, I would need to learn a lot more about this thing called blogging.

Before I jumped into bed that night, I decided to make one last entry in my so-called private blog. This time I was much more cautious. I made sure to change my name so there would be no chance anyone could ever figure out who had written it. My evening entry closed with the following prayer:

> *Now I lay me down to sleep*
> *I pray thee, Lord, my blog to keep*
> *A secret 'til my dying day*
> *Or at least until I find a way*
> *To share and only do my part*
> *Stay close, dear Lord, and heal my heart.*
> *Amen*

The Healing Power of Laughter

When all was said and done, the experience of writing my first blog provided me and a few others with some much-needed comic relief. I learned through this that I could laugh and not take myself too seriously. Following the pain of divorce, this medicine was just what the doctor ordered.

Laughter is a gift God gave us that helps us cope in the hard seasons of life. Unfortunately, those times are often when we feel most alone, and laughter can be the furthest thing from our minds. Nehemiah 8:10 says "the joy of the LORD is your strength." That means without joy, our resilience wanes and our strength fails, leaving us vulnerable and depleted. Genuine joy, on the other hand, sustains us in adversity and helps us navigate life's trials.

In 1964, Norman Cousins, a well-known editor for the *Saturday Review*, was diagnosed with a degenerative disease that caused the breakdown of collagen in his body. This illness left him immobilized with severe pain, fever, and near paralysis of his back, neck, and legs. Told by his doctor that only one in five hundred people ever fully recovered, Cousins determined he would be the one to beat those odds. And beat them he did.

While confined to a New York hospital bed, Cousins took an unconventional approach to healing. He persuaded the nurses to play reruns of the classic comedy TV show *Candid Camera*. In addition to conventional medicine, Cousins tapped into his body's natural resources and boosted his immune system with laughter. Deciding the hospital was no place for a sick person who wanted to get well, and with the approval of his doctor, Cousins checked himself into a hotel room, where he continued his laughter regimen.

Amazingly, he found that just ten minutes of deep belly laughs had an anesthetic effect that would lead to two hours of pain-free sleep. Whenever the laughter's effects wore off, Cousins would switch on his projector again. Through his unique approach, he made a remarkable recovery, demonstrating the profound connection between mind and body. Cousins later returned to work and went on to live a full life.[1]

> Laughter is a gift God gave us that helps us cope in the hard seasons of life.

What Cousins discovered about laughter's healing qualities only proved that what the Word of God says is true: A merry heart is as healthy for our body as good medicine (Prov. 17:22). Just like medicine, laughter reduces stress levels, fights off depression, lowers blood pressure, sends dopamine (the feel-good chemical) to our brain, and prevents disease, helping us live longer.

Take a moment and look in the mirror. Have you lost your joy? Are you having a hard time seeing past your current circumstances? If so, know that you are not alone. God sees you and cares so very much about you. He sees the pain you try so hard to keep hidden so no one else will see. You might be able to hide it from others, but be assured that you cannot hide it from God. More than anything, your heavenly Father wants you to let Him into that hurting space and allow Him to help you hold the heavy things you carry:

Are you tired? Worn out? Burned out on religion? Come to me. Get away with me and you'll recover your life. I'll show you how to take a real rest. Walk with me and work with me—watch how

I do it. Learn the unforced rhythms of grace. I won't lay anything heavy or ill-fitting on you. Keep company with me and you'll learn to live freely and lightly. (Matt. 11:28–30 MSG)

Even though the last thing you might feel like doing right now is laughing, make an intentional decision to laugh *despite your feelings*. That's right, *choose* to laugh even if you don't feel like it. Ask God to give you a gift of laughter. As Sarah declared in Genesis 21:6, "God has brought me laughter, and everyone who hears about this will laugh with me."

The Power of Agreement

When I was growing up, my parents always emphasized three things in our family: First, that it was essential to show our love and to laugh together. Second, they taught us to have goals and dreams for our future. And third, they modeled the importance of committing our goals and plans to God in prayer.

Not only were we encouraged to have goals, but my dad also stressed the importance of writing them down. As a child, I used to dread the end of the year because I knew I would be asked, "What are your short-term and long-term goals for the upcoming year?" Those are some pretty big orders for a little girl who, at the time, barely knew what she would be doing in the next hour.

Old habits die hard, though, because it was now late December 2016, and I found myself writing one specific end-of-year goal in my journal: *If the sky is the limit, I would like to begin dating again in 2017.*

Just the thought of dating was daunting. It had been over twenty-seven years since I dated anyone other than my ex-husband. Despite how big and ridiculous my new goal felt, I secretly wrote it down. Having committed to my goal by writing it down, I knew it was time to pray.

The Bible is filled with instructions about the power of prayer. We are even given examples of how to pray. One such instruction is found in Matthew 18:18–20, where Jesus says, "Again I say to you, that if two believers on earth agree [that is, are of one mind, in harmony] about anything that they ask [within the will of God], it will be done for them by My Father in heaven. For where two or three are gathered in My name [meeting together as My followers], I am there among them" (AMP).

When I was growing up, it was not unusual for my parents to ask me and my siblings if there was anything they could agree with us in prayer about. So it seemed only fitting for me to ask my parents to pray and agree that the right man would find his way into my life. I broached the subject one day when I went to their house and we sat together in their kitchen.

"Mom and Dad, I think I'm ready for a relationship again," I sheepishly began.

Before I could utter another word, my dad reached across the table and grabbed my hand and my mother's hand. "Lord, Kim wants a husband," he began to pray. "Dorothy and I join our faith with hers and ask that you grant her the desires of her heart."

I honestly can't say I remember much of anything else that was said, but I left their home knowing God had heard our prayers.

Fishers of Men

By now it was the beginning of 2017. It had been almost four years since my divorce. My oldest two children were already married and living on their own, and my youngest two children would soon be leaving for college. During the past four years, I had been careful to keep my promise of solely focusing on my children, but the time had come for me to focus on myself.

It was a Saturday morning, about a month after I had prayed with my parents at their kitchen table. I was alone in the house and was busy vacuuming and cleaning when I suddenly heard what can only be described as an inner voice speaking to my heart: *You're going to be married by the end of this year. It will go fast. You need to buckle your seat belt!*

Unsure what to think, I wondered if I had just made this up in my mind. Not wanting to appear foolish, I decided to keep this information to myself. If what I heard was true, time would surely tell.

A few days later my oldest daughter called me on the phone. She was going to be in my neighborhood and asked if she could stop by for a visit. Like most mothers, I get excited whenever there's an opportunity for me to see one of my children. She arrived, and we greeted each other with a hug.

"Mom, have you ever considered the possibility of online dating?" she asked with a smile. "You and Dad have been divorced four years now, and maybe it's time you moved on."

Her question caught me off guard since up until this time I had not even mentioned the subject of dating to any of my children. Just the idea of dating (let alone *online* dating) overwhelmed me. She saw the look of terror on my face and reassured me with a smile before continuing.

"There's nothing to it, Mom. I can help you."

With that, she opened my laptop and began to search dating sites we had seen advertised on TV many times. After locating what appeared to be a reputable site, the first step was to come up with a profile name. It could be any name of my choosing, but I needed to keep in mind that it would be what potential matches saw when they looked at my picture.

"How about Kim3162?" I suggested. At age fifty, I knew I needed something I could easily remember, so I chose my first name followed by the first four digits of my house address. Laughing at my naivete, my daughter convinced me it might not be the most brilliant idea to give so much of my personal information away to strangers I didn't know.

"How about calling yourself 'I Can't Cook'?" she teased. (Leave it to a wise-cracking daughter!) We finally settled on a profile name that sounded whimsical and fun.

Sheesh! It had taken more than an hour just to create my profile name. By now, my interest and energy were waning. The next step was to write an introductory paragraph that described who I was and what I was looking for in a relationship. My daughter was not amused when I suggested something like "I have all my shots and am spayed and dewormed. Original owner just changed his mind. I am looking to be rehomed." Even though I thoroughly entertained myself with this idea, I decided against it since I could only imagine the type of responses this intro might draw.

Saying this process felt a little desperate and humiliating would be a gross understatement. I was reminded of the popular sitcom *Welcome Back Kotter* that I used to watch in high school. Whenever Mr. Kotter asked a question to his classroom full of under-performing students, a nerdy, gangly boy named Arnold Horshack would flail his arm in the air, begging, "Oh, oh, oh, pick me! Pick me!" This was exactly how I felt as I wrote my online profile. It felt intimidating, like it was up to me to convince a man why I was worthy of his time and attention.

When I completed writing and rewriting (and rewriting) my profile, I clicked the Submit button. Phew! I'd done it!

Oh, my goodness! What had I just done?

Before I could change my mind, my daughter announced it was time for her to head home.

You should know something about me: I've always been a bit of a risk-taker. Now that I had committed to online dating, I decided to get even braver.

In my teen years, I spent many summers at a remote fishing camp my parents owned in northern Canada. I learned that to catch a fish, you have to put your line in the water. The more lines you have in the water, the better your chances of catching a fish. Can you see where I am going with this?

Hmmm . . . why wouldn't this same strategy apply here? If registering on one dating site is good, I bet registering on FIVE dating sites would be even better.

So, within a few short hours, that's precisely what I did. I was determined to increase the odds of finding my perfect match. Now all I had to do was sit back and wait.

Each morning, I hesitantly opened my computer to see if anyone had reached out to contact me. It took only a few weeks and a few conversations before I agreed to meet one of the matches for dinner at a restaurant.

Friday night arrived before I knew it. Like a schoolgirl, I panicked as I tried on outfit after outfit, determined to make an excellent first impression. My nerves were on edge, and I worried I was making a mistake. *What will I say? Will he even like me? What if he tries to kiss me at the end of our date?* These were just a few of the questions that popped into my mind.

My youngest children were home on college break and my older two had stopped by for a visit. They all sensed my uneasiness as I got ready, and soon I became the fodder for their lighthearted banter. The proverbial shoe was now on the other foot. They teased and lovingly mocked me while giving me the same "talk" I had so often given them, saying things like, "Mom, do you know how far is 'too far' to go on a date?" and "We expect you home by curfew!"

I rolled my eyes and picked up my car keys as I headed for the front door. I hadn't even reached it before one of my children felt the need to shout a last-minute warning.

"You know, Mom, I've heard there's a black market for body organs. People have been found in bathtubs full of ice with their organs cut out of them." My kids giggled when they saw my eyes get as large as saucers. "We're just kidding!" they said with a wink. And with that, I headed out the door.

The restaurant I chose was packed when I arrived. A polite hostess came to greet me.

"Are you meeting someone here?" she asked.

My face flushed as I leaned in close, embarrassed to whisper my answer.

"I'm meeting someone here for the very first time," I confessed in a hushed voice. Oh, how I hoped no one could overhear. The hostess flashed a knowing smile and told me my party had already been seated.

"Right this way," she said and led me to a nearby booth where a nice-looking man stood up and extended his hand in my direction.

"Hi! You must be Kim."

Before long, we were engaged in pleasant conversation. The evening was going well, and I finally felt myself relaxing. Just then a muffled buzzing sound came from the direction of my purse. I recognized the vibration of my cell phone.

"I'm so sorry," I apologized. My hand fumbled around in my purse. Grabbing my phone, I checked to see who was calling. A smile spread over my face, and I couldn't hold back a chuckle. Staring back at me was a text message from one of my children that read "#SaveYourKidneys!!!"

The evening ended, and we gave each other a warm hug; however, we agreed we were not a true connection. Though I hadn't found love, I walked away with newfound confidence. I recognized that while life had brought some unexpected turns and hadn't always been easy, it had definitely not passed me by. I had a choice to make: I could either pick myself up, dust myself off, and get back in the proverbial saddle. Or I could stay home, nurse my wounds, and observe life from a distance like a spectator. I knew I had adventures and possibilities waiting around the corner for me. My part was to push past my fear of the unknown.

Embracing Laughter and Joy

Stepping outside your comfort zone can be intimidating. Unless you are willing to do something different, you risk staying stuck in the same spot. I knew if I wanted to find love again, I had to be willing to do my part. That meant making myself discoverable while trusting God to do the rest.

Signing up for online dating felt like a big risk for me. But risks can look like a number of different things. In my office, for example, I regularly work with teenage clients who struggle with the heaviness of depression, anxiety, and other significant issues that even most adults have a hard time coping with. A practice I began long ago is to end our sessions by instructing them to pick one of their favorite songs from their music playlist and play it as loud as they can while I set a timer for thirty seconds. When they're ready, we stand up, kick off our shoes, and begin to dance.

The wide-eyed look I receive the first time we do this is priceless. But it soon becomes every teen client's favorite part of our session. They can't believe that Miss Kim would actually get up and dance with them. Uninhibited (and more than a little uncoordinated), we throw caution to the wind as we shake off the heaviness of the preceding hour.

I know what you're probably thinking right now: *But I thought you said you don't like to dance!*

While it's true I get incredibly self-conscious when someone is watching me, something happens when I dance with my teenage clients. We let loose with freedom, silliness, and laughter. If you were a fly on the wall, you would see me perform the Swim, the Twist, jumping jacks, and any other crazy move I can think of. The result? My teen clients get to experience a moment of laughter and joy in the midst of their pain.

> Even amid sorrow and pain, we can find sweet moments of joy and laughter if we look hard enough.

My teen clients aren't the only ones who have experienced pain. I see clients of all ages who have faced many kinds of struggle and heartbreak. I am often asked, "Is it okay to laugh, even when I'm sad and going through a hard time?" My answer is that laughter is not only permissible; it is often a necessary and powerful tool for healing. Laughter doesn't discount the fact that we're in pain; it simply makes the pain more tolerable. They are not mutually exclusive.

Take me for example. The end of my marriage was not the way I imagined my life would go. Nor was the attack I described in the opening chapter. But I've learned that even amid sorrow and pain, we can find sweet moments of joy and laughter if we look hard enough. For me, those moments were most often found in a friend's warm smile, my family's unconditional love, and a renewed hope that God still promised a good future for me. Those were the moments that told me I was ready to embrace that future and shake off the heaviness that had overshadowed me for way too long.

You deserve to have all these experiences too. So, for just a moment, pretend you are in one of my teenage therapy sessions. I invite you to get ready and set your timer because here comes my personal thirty-second dance. Picture me in my office dancing like nobody's watching and inviting you to join the laughter party. Why? Because joy is not just a luxury, it's a necessity—especially amid life's storms.

PAUSE AND REFLECT

- What in your life feels heavy right now that you need to permit yourself to shake off, even if just for a short while? This may be the time to move out of your sorrow and begin to make yourself laugh on purpose. Even if it feels fake, do it. If you need some help getting started, try watching YouTube videos of babies laughing. Put on your favorite comedian. Watch reruns of favorite shows that have tickled your funny bone in the past. Laughter is both healing and contagious.

- Having friends who support us through difficult times is crucial. Prioritizing friendships that bring joy and positivity fosters resilience and makes navigating life's challenges more manageable. Surrounding ourselves with friends who uplift and encourage personal growth is essential, while also being mindful of relationships that may hinder our progress. Take a moment to reflect on the friends you surround yourself with. Are they sources of encouragement and laughter, or do they contribute to stress and negativity? Be willing to reevaluate whether your friendships align with your needs, particularly during times of crisis. (See "The Power of Friendship" in Tools for Growth and Healing.)

- Finally, I invite you to be just like my teenage clients. That's right, pick your favorite fast song, turn it loud, set your timer for thirty seconds, and get up and dance. Choose to put on a garment of praise. Come on . . . I dare you!

PRAYER OF OUR HEART

Father, just like Sarah in the Bible, I ask You to bring back my laughter. In the hard places where I have lost touch with my joy, help me see Your goodness and find the strength to smile again. Bring godly friendships my way as encouragement and help me be the kind of person who sows encouragement in others. Your Word says that Your joy will bring me strength. Thank You for strengthening my weary heart. In Jesus's name I pray. Amen.

4

A TIME TO HOPE

It's Too Soon to Give Up!

Hope is faith holding out its hand in the dark.

GEORGE ILES

Now to Him who is able to do exceedingly abundantly above all
that we ask or think, according to the power that works in us,
to Him be glory in the church by Christ Jesus to all generations,
forever and ever. Amen.

EPHESIANS 3:20–21 NKJV

I am often asked why I chose to become a licensed therapist. My answer always begins the same way: There was a time in my life when I had lost all hope and desperately needed someone to steer me back to it.

Two years into my marriage, major problems crept in. Though we sought help, the ongoing counsel we received felt more like putting a Band-Aid on what had become a gaping wound. During these times of despair, I made a vow to myself that one day I would find a way to go back to school, receive the necessary education, and become a licensed counselor. I determined I would become a hope-giver to others who, like me, felt all hope was gone.

And so began my journey. At the age of thirty-seven, with four children under the age of ten, I enrolled in online classes to fulfill the requirements for a bachelor's degree I had started before I got married. For the next several years, my routine would be to safely tuck my children into bed each night, break out my schoolbooks, and begin studying. I often stayed up until the wee hours of the morning, writing papers and cramming for upcoming tests. Sleep became a luxury I could barely afford, yet somehow I managed to have just enough energy to make it through another day.

When I finally had enough college credits to graduate with my bachelor's degree, I immediately enrolled in a master's program. It took another two years before I was ready to enter the counseling profession. There were many times I wasn't sure I would ever finish my goal. But my persistence paid off, and the day came when

I proudly crossed the finish line with my degree in marriage and family therapy.

Now, twenty-one years after I first found myself at a place of despair in my marriage, I found myself facing a similar feeling of hopelessness. This time, it was about whether I could ever find love again at my age. Even though I told myself I was done with online dating, my curiosity got the better of me, and I couldn't resist peeking in on the dating sites I was now a member of.

I came to have a love/hate relationship with these sites since they had an uncanny way of affecting my self-esteem for good and bad. On good days, I'd be entertained and find myself giggling at some of the suggestions for my "perfect" match. On bad days, I took personal offense at some of the selections and wondered if somehow, somewhere, someone was playing a cruel joke on me. Some days it was hard to not take things personally. During those times, words my dad had spoken in my late teen years came back to haunt me and echoed in my mind: "Kim, don't ask God for a ten if you're an eight."

Stop the bus! Why in the world would anyone tell a young and impressionable girl this?

As an adult, I've come to understand that my father's words, though a bit misguided, stemmed from a place of love. At the time he said them, I, like every other teenage girl in high school, had my heart set on the most popular, handsome, star athlete boy in school. I was the shy, overweight girl with two crooked front teeth, an awkward laugh, and extremely low self-esteem. In the eyes of the popular boys, I was invisible.

Now, my father loved me very much, and he didn't want to see his little girl get hurt. His intention was to protect me from potential rejection. When he said I was an eight, he wasn't trying to put me down. He wasn't thinking like a teenage girl; he was thinking like a dad who wanted to keep his daughter safe. He didn't realize how his words might make me feel.

Even now, I cringe as I think about the impact these words had on the value I assigned to my worth when growing up. In my mind, being a ten meant you were beautiful, desired by others, and worthy of love. If I was only an eight, that must mean I was less than, pitiful, and that no one would ever want me. This experience underscored for me the profound impact words can have.

Words Can Be Hope-Stealers or Hope-Givers

Whether intentional or not, words can steal our hope away. The old adage "Sticks and stones can break my bones, but words will never hurt me" couldn't be any further from the truth! Words are some of the most powerful weapons we have in our arsenal. They can cut like a knife, leaving deep, gaping wounds that, for many, last a lifetime.

As a therapist, I frequently encounter clients whose lives have been deeply impacted by negative messages ingrained during child-hood. Over time, these messages solidify into beliefs that persist into adulthood. These beliefs echo messages such as, "I'm worthless, unlovable, invisible, at fault, unforgivable, less than, damaged, unwanted, a nuisance, or not good enough."

Much like the voicemail function on a cell phone, our hearts become receptacles for these negative messages. When we receive them, we face a choice:

- We can *play* the message.
- We can *replay* the message.
- We can *save* the message.
- We can *delete* the message.

Unfortunately, rather than deleting these harmful messages from our heart voicemail, we often choose, both consciously and subconsciously, to replay the negativity over and over again. If that wasn't bad enough, we choose to save it again for later. Over time, these messages get indelibly etched into our minds and hearts, shaping our identities for years to come.

The good news is we don't have to keep replaying the lies and damaging beliefs. By filtering them through the lens of God's truth, we can learn to discern their falsehood and reject them. If God's Word says it, you can believe it. Any message that contradicts God's affirmations about our worth and identity needs to be deleted. Our response should be an adamant "Wrong number!" as we hang up the phone. Just as we wouldn't entertain spam phone calls, we must treat negative messages that steal our hope as spam and refuse to give them any attention. Recognizing Satan's role as both a scam artist and a spam artist, we must reject his narratives and cling to the truth of God's Word about our identity in Christ.

> Any message that contradicts God's affirmations about our worth and identity needs to be deleted.

Many years ago, when my son was seven years old, he came home from school crying one day. When I asked what was wrong, he said he had been laughed at by kids who told him he had "vampire teeth." His teeth were quite normal at the time, and the kids were just being cruel in the way that kids can be.

Burying his head in his sweet little hands, his shoulders shook as his cries turned into inconsolable sobs.

Scooping him up in my arms, I asked, "Son, what does God say about you?"

Looking up at me through his big crocodile tears, he hiccuped out his answer.

"God says He has plans for me . . . and they're big!"

My mama heart smiled.

"That's right, son. God has good plans for you. And they are big!"

Have you, like me or my son, had words spoken over you that continue to ring out time and time again? Words that make you doubt your value. Words that leave your heart bleeding. Are there words and messages that need to be uprooted in your life?

Though words can destroy, they can also be like honey and act as a healing balm to soothe, repair, and encourage. Proverbs 18:21 states, "The tongue can bring death or life; those who love to talk will reap the consequences" (NLT).

Thirty-five years after the idea was planted in my heart that I was "only an 8," I had sat next to my parents at their kitchen table and told them I was ready to be in a relationship again. That was the day we joined hands to pray and asked God to grant my heart's desire for a mate.

A few short days later, I heard a knock at my door.

Peeking through the window, I saw it was my dad, and he was holding something behind his back. I opened the door, and he handed me a gift bag. His face beamed as he watched me reach in to see what was inside. I riffled through the tissue paper until my fingers closed around something rectangular and hard. Pulling it out, I discovered a book titled *You Are a Prize to Be Won* by Wendy Griffith, popular cohost of *The 700 Club*.

In her book, Ms. Griffith shares her personal journey of overcoming heartache and finding solace in God's love. Through her narrative, she empowers women to reclaim their intrinsic worth and recognize their immeasurable value.

My eyes brimmed with tears when I opened the front cover and recognized my dad's scribbled words:

> Believe God for a gift of faith. You are one in 10,000! You deserve it! Accept it! And don't question it! Love, Dad

Those words that my dad had innocently spoken years earlier and that had impacted me so negatively were now replaced with words that spoke of love and life. As you read this, think back to words that have been spoken to you and left your heart hurting. Would you join me in asking Jesus to replace those hurtful words the enemy has used against you time and time again with His words of truth about you? Listen closely. Can you hear the voice of our heavenly Father wooing you?

I can't tell you exactly what God would say to you. But given what Scripture says, I believe it would sound something like this. Take a moment and receive His letter of love to your heart right now.

My precious, precious daughter,

I planned you before the world began and saw you as you were being formed in utter seclusion. I still see you. I see how many hairs are on your head. I see every tear you shed. I know when your foot slips and you begin to stumble or fall. Do you realize just how precious you are to Me? Your face is imprinted on the palm of My hand and I am always, ALWAYS, thinking about you. My thoughts for you outnumber the tiniest grains of sand that stretch out by the ocean. If you listen closely enough, you will hear Me singing a love song over you. You are My masterpiece! No one else I ever created is exactly like you, and I did that on purpose. You are My prize, and I want you to know how very much I love you. You are a prize to be cherished.

Love,
Your heavenly Father

Identifying Hope Builders

The Greek word for "hope" is *elpis*.[1] It means "to look forward with pleasurable confidence and expectation." Hope says, "Things can change." Hope says, "It's not over yet!" Hope is future-oriented and looks for possibilities.

While hopelessness keeps us stuck, hope pulls us forward.

While hopelessness fuels defeat, hope motivates us to action and strengthens our resolve.

When hopelessness cries, "What if things don't work out?" hope shouts, "What if it is beyond your wildest dreams?"

Hopelessness relies on our feelings. Hope is born from our expectations and relies on faith.

The easiest way to build hope is to get your eyes off your circumstances and onto Jesus. Instead of focusing on the details of "how?" and "when?" focus on the "who" of Jesus. In 2 Timothy 1:12 Paul states, "I know whom I have believed, and am convinced that he is able to guard what I have entrusted to him until that day." We need to believe that God is not only able but also willing. Romans 8:28 reassures us that God has a plan and makes all things work together for our good.

> Don't wait for someone else to encourage you. Learn to encourage yourself.

Another way we can build hope is by learning to challenge our way of thinking. Don't wait for someone else to encourage you. Learn to encourage yourself. Don't sit and have a pity party, fixating on everything that has gone wrong or not turned out the way you wanted. Talk yourself into victory. As David declares in Psalm 43:5, "Why, my soul, are you downcast? Why so disturbed within me? Put your hope in God, for I will yet praise him, my Savior and my God." We're also told that when David was at his lowest, he "encouraged himself" in the Lord his God (1 Sam. 30:6 KJV).

The Bible is full of stories about people who faced insurmountable odds yet still clung to hope. Joseph held on to hope when he was unfairly thrown into prison (Gen. 39). The woman who had suffered for twelve years from an issue of blood held on to the hope that if she could just touch Jesus, she would be healed (Luke 8:43). Naaman the leper had hope that if he dipped in the Jordan River, his leprosy would be cleansed (2 Kings 5). God gave us these stories as an example of what expectant hope can do. When we remember the miracles God performed in the Bible and the ways He has shown up for us in our own lives, our faith is fueled and becomes strong.

In Joshua 4 we read how the Israelites crossed the Jordan River into the promised land. God instructed Joshua to select twelve men, one from each tribe of Israel, to gather twelve stones from the middle of the river and set them up as a permanent monument to remind future generations of God's miraculous deliverance. In verses 21–24, Joshua tells the Israelites:

> In the future when your descendants ask their parents, "What do these stones mean?" tell them, "Israel crossed the Jordan on dry ground." For the LORD your God dried up the Jordan before you until you had crossed over. The LORD your God did to the Jordan what he had done to the Red Sea when he dried it up before us until we had crossed over. He did this so that all the peoples of the earth might know that the hand of the LORD is powerful and so that you might always fear the LORD your God.

> **Rediscovering hope not only makes the challenges we face bearable but also sets the stage for believing that circumstances can indeed change.**

The twelve stones were a tangible reminder to the Israelites of God's faithfulness. We, too, can strengthen our expectancy by recalling the ways in which God has shown up for us in the past. When we stop to rehearse His goodness in our lives, our belief in God's promises is reinforced.

Because of our humanness, there are moments in life when hope seems just out of reach and the desire to give up weighs heavy on our hearts. During these times, I want to encourage you to reach out to God and ask Him to give you a gift of faith to reignite your hope once more. Rediscovering hope not only makes the challenges we face bearable but also sets the stage for believing that circumstances can indeed change.

Finding Hope

Like I said, when it came to dating, I had reached a point where hope was waning. Despite three months of actively seeking the right person, I felt like nothing was changing. The prospect of finding love through online dating seemed increasingly dim. I still believed the message I felt the Lord had spoken to my heart about me being married by the end of the year, I just doubted it was going to happen this way. I decided to cancel my dating site membership, but before I did, I agreed to meet one last man for breakfast. In that moment, I reasoned, what did I have to lose?

The morning of April 1 arrived. April Fool's Day. I cautioned myself to temper my expectations. When I pulled up to the diner's front door, my heart skipped a beat at the sight of a tall and very handsome man waiting outside. His smile was warm and welcoming, and something about him drew my attention—as if he had been expectantly watching and waiting for me his whole life.

"Hi, I'm Andrew," he said with a broad grin, extending his hand to greet me.

Over the next two hours, time seemed to stand still as we engaged in lively conversation, exchanging laughter and stories with a natural ease. At one point, our animated interaction caught the attention of an elderly couple sitting nearby who couldn't resist discreetly observing our infectious energy. It was evident we were providing great amusement.

Reluctantly, we drew our breakfast date to a close. Neither of us wanted the morning to end. Not knowing what else to do, we awkwardly hugged and said our goodbyes before I got in my car. What was it about this man that made me smile from ear to ear? I couldn't help but wonder if I would hear from him again. I realized I truly hoped I would.

Within hours, Andrew reached out. His name flashing across my screen sent a rush of excitement through me. I didn't want to appear too eager, so I let it ring a few more times before answering. I held my breath, and the warm voice on the other end began to speak.

"Hi again! This is Andrew. I was thinking . . . [long pause] . . . would you want to go out with me again tomorrow evening?"

It didn't take much convincing, and I happily agreed to meet him again. Why was I feeling so giddy? I couldn't remember the last time I felt this nervous and excited all at the same time. The next evening, I arrived at the restaurant where Andrew was already sitting. Once again, he greeted me with a broad, boyish grin. I laughed when he told me how he had worn his skinny jeans to impress me but now could barely breathe. His laughter filled the room, and something inside me knew I was finally "home."

As our relationship blossomed over the following weeks, Andrew and I saw each other every chance we got. We met for early breakfast, snuck in a quick lunch here and there, and many evenings he had supper waiting at his house after a long day of work.

One evening, as I snuggled close beside him, Andrew appeared nervous. He had a serious look on his face. He hesitated, then slowly began to speak.

"Yesterday, I asked Google how long you have to know someone before you can be sure you're actually in love." This was the last thing I ever expected him to say. I held my breath and waited for him to continue.

Looking deeply into my eyes, he said, "You know, I want to marry you."

Andrew's unexpected confession stirred a whirlwind of emotions within me. I knew I had been falling in love with Andrew with each passing day. I had even cautiously allowed my heart to entertain the idea that maybe—just maybe—this could be the man I had been waiting for. Since Andrew's declaration of wanting to marry me was not exactly a question awaiting an answer, I decided to play it safe. I smiled and simply remained quiet.

When Hope Is Threatened

Even as I dared to imagine the possibility of a promising future with Andrew, a part of me wrestled with quiet doubts. Despite having made the decision to leave my ex-husband behind, the prospect of fully embracing this new chapter filled me with apprehension. My desire to please God remained my utmost priority. More than anything, I wanted reassurance I was not disappointing God with my decision to walk away from my ex-husband. In the midst of this inner turmoil, one thing was sure: Being with Andrew felt undeniably right. In his presence I experienced a happiness unlike any other, and I didn't want to let that feeling go. After careful reflection, I finally reconciled within myself that walking away didn't mean I was doing something wrong in God's eyes.

Just four weeks into my relationship with Andrew, my ex-husband reached out, suggesting we discuss a matter concerning our children. His request for me to swing by his apartment after work didn't strike me as unusual. Since our divorce, we had maintained an amicable relationship and occasionally shared a meal while discussing the welfare of our children. As reluctant as I was, I agreed to his request.

When I arrived at my ex-husband's apartment, he was busy in the kitchen putting the finishing touches on a dinner he had made. The aromas coming from the oven and the growl of my stomach reminded me I had not eaten since morning.

"What did you want to talk about?" I asked.

"There's plenty of time to talk. Let's wait until after dinner," he said with a smile. With that, he began carrying food to the table he had already set for two.

Although tired from my long workday and antsy to get home, I reluctantly agreed to stay. The conversation remained light throughout dinner; however, as the evening progressed, the tone of the conversation took an unexpected turn.

"You know, since our divorce I've put in a lot of work on myself," he began earnestly. "I've become a man I believe you could be proud of. But you won't really see that unless you give me another chance to prove it by spending more time together."

A quick glance at my expression was all it took for my ex-husband to realize his words were falling on deaf ears. Getting up from the table, I made my way to the living room where he followed close behind me.

"It's too late," I asserted firmly. "I'm involved with someone else now, and it's becoming serious. You've had your opportunity, but it's time you accepted that it's over. You need to begin building a life for yourself—one that doesn't include me."

My ex-husband bristled and his shoulders straightened. His chest puffed out and his voice became louder. He closed the physical distance between us as he took another step toward me. A sense of unease washed over me—a feeling I hadn't experienced before in my interactions with him.

"Well, maybe I'll just have to go and have a talk with this man!" he exclaimed, his tone carrying an unfamiliar edge of threat. The dark intensity in his eyes deepened, and the uneasy feeling in my stomach continued to grow. Realizing this was a departure from our usual dynamic, I knew it was time to take action and leave.

"I'm done," I firmly stated. "We're through, and you need to move on!" My eyes scanned the apartment for where I had set my oversized purse. Grabbing it, I swung the door open and didn't look back. His bitter words followed me into the night.

"Sure! Run like you always do!"

The angry words were flung like poison arrows in my direction. Though they were not an overt threat, his demeanor at dinner and what he'd said about Andrew unnerved me. For the first time I could remember, fear for my safety entered my mind.

My heart pounding, I quickly made my way down the two flights of stairs to the parking lot where my car waited to take me to safety.

Click. The sound of my car door locking safely behind me brought an immediate sense of relief. My hands trembled as I shoved the key into the ignition. Any sense of safety I previously felt was gone. All I knew was I had to get out of there.

Ultimately, I knew I was in no state of mind to go home or be alone, so I decided to dial Andrew's number.

"Hey, would it be okay if I stopped by for a while?" I asked, attempting to sound nonchalant.

The reassuring voice on the other end of the line was all I needed. My panicky mind settled, and I set out on my journey. When I finally pulled into Andrew's driveway, it was nine o'clock.

"I won't stay long," I promised. "I just wanted to be able to see you."

Wrapping myself in Andrew's gentle embrace, I hesitantly shared the events of my evening. Tears welled up in my eyes as I recounted my ex-husband's words about maybe needing to pay Andrew a visit. I explained that this veiled threat meant my ex-husband might call or try to harass him at work. Worst-case scenario, he might try to sabotage our relationship by spreading ridiculous lies about me. Never in a million years did I imagine Andrew's physical safety might be at risk. Still, the emotional toll of the threat weighed heavily on my mind.

"Andrew . . . would you fight for me?" I timidly asked. Holding my breath, I hoped and prayed for the answer I wanted.

A grin broke across his face and he kissed my forehead.

"Of course I would!" His words comforted me as he pulled me even closer to him.

"How can you sound so sure?" I questioned, still wanting more reassurance.

Andrew chuckled at my insistence and replied with a voice full of optimism, "Because, sweetheart, you are worth fighting for!"

By now, it was almost eleven o'clock and time for me to head home. My heart was settled and at peace. We walked to my car, and Andrew kissed me goodnight, reminding me of his promise to always fight for me. The significance our parting words would come to hold was beyond anything I could have foreseen.

In less than nine hours, Andrew would not only be engaging in the fight *of* his life but in a literal fight *for* his life. His commitment to me would soon be put to the ultimate test.

PAUSE AND REFLECT

- Think back to a time when hurtful words were spoken to you that got planted and rooted in your heart. What were these words, and who spoke them? What has been the lasting effect of these words? Maybe for you it wasn't the words spoken to you; instead, it was the words that were never spoken to you but that your heart longed to hear. Words such as "I love you," "I'm so very proud of you," or even "You did such a great job!" Take a moment and ask God to rewrite the old messages on your heart to reflect His truth and what He says about you.

- What are the things you have been believing God for? What are the secret desires of your heart? Has it taken longer than you think for those desires or dreams to materialize? Have you lost your sense of hope? If so, pray and ask God to stir those desires up inside you once again. Ask Him to give you reassurance to know that your desires and dreams matter to Him too.

- An effective strategy for building hope is to pause and reflect on both the big and small ways in which God has shown His presence and faithfulness in your life. Similar to how the Israelites erected a tangible reminder of God's faithfulness, take a moment and write down a physical reminder of instances when God has shown you His provision, guidance, and faithfulness.

PRAYER OF OUR HEART

Father, I ask that You take the enemy's lies I have believed about myself for so long and replace them with Your words of truth about me. Help me receive Your unconditional love so I can begin to see myself the same way You do. Your Word says the things that matter to me also matter to You. I ask You to stir up the secret dreams and desires You planted in my heart once again. Resurrect my hopes and fuel my determination to hold on until I see them come to pass. In Your mighty name I pray. Amen.

A TIME TO WEEP

Going Through the Valley

God is not only the God of the mountain, but He is also present
in the valley.

BILLY GRAHAM

> Even when I walk
> through the dark valley of death,
> I will not be afraid,
> for you are close beside me.
> Your rod and your staff
> protect and comfort me.
>
> PSALM 23:4 NLT

I went to bed shortly after eleven o'clock, but something inside me felt very uneasy and told me to lock my bedroom door. I had spent many nights alone in the house since my youngest children had gone off to college, but for some reason this time felt different. I decided not to question this feeling and got out of bed. The inner button of my doorknob quietly clicked beneath the pressure of my touch. I knew I was safe inside my bedroom and returned to the king-sized bed that welcomed me each night. Freshly washed sheets that smelled of lavender made it easy to snuggle deeply beneath my down-filled comforter. Before long, my eyelids began to droop. I drifted off to sleep.

Without warning, I woke with a jolt to the sound of my bedroom door crashing to the floor and an angry voice screaming obscenities at me. The warm blanket that moments before had swaddled me in comfort was now a barrier I gripped to my chest. My eyes, still groggy from sleep, strained to see where the thundering commotion was coming from. It took just a few short seconds before it registered. The angry face glaring back at me belonged to the man I had once been married to for twenty-three years.

Clearly intoxicated, my ex-husband staggered in the direction of my bed. His hand shakily gripped a gun that was leveled at my chest. His slurred words sent chills of disbelief racing up and down my spine.

"I've just come from killing your parents!"

The magnitude of his words registered in my brain. For a brief moment I envisioned the bodies of my elderly parents lying somewhere in a pool of their blood. My mind wondered what it must have been like in their last tormenting moments of life. My close relationship with my parents had always been a source of contention between my ex-husband and me. He knew if there was one way he could hurt me, this would be it.

What could I have done to protect them?

I firmly ordered myself to remain calm. I needed to keep my wits about me. If what he said was true, there was nothing I could do for my parents now. My immediate focus had to be on getting myself out of impending danger. I would have to grieve this loss later.

Snap out of it, Kim! Just stay alive! I told myself. *Whatever you do, don't do anything that will antagonize him!*

My heart pounded harder and harder. I watched as his steps brought him closer and closer to my side.

"Get out of bed!" he hissed and grabbed the hair at the base of my neck.

Before I knew what was happening, the cold steel of a gun barrel rammed past my front teeth and forced its way to the back of my throat, making me gag. Tears welled in my eyes, and I watched his finger shake on the trigger.

Please, dear God . . . Oh please don't let me die! I silently begged. *My children need me! Dear God . . . please, oh please . . .*

The gun that had been lodged in my mouth was now shoved against my throat. I struggled for air and knew I wouldn't last much longer.

My fingernails dug into the hand holding me captive. No matter how hard I tried, my frantic attempts to relieve the pressure on my throat only made matters worse and fueled the smoldering anger I saw in my ex-husband's face.

The room seemed to swirl about me in nauseating circles. I knew it would not be long before I lost consciousness from lack of oxygen. I had no time to waste. I had to think fast!

While one of my hands frantically grabbed at the gun digging into my neck, the other pushed against my ex-husband's body.

Gathering every ounce of strength I could muster, I pushed as hard as I could to get away. The imbalance in our sizes caused us to stumble backward, and with a thud I landed on top of him on the floor. In a quick turn of events, I was now the one in control. Instinctively, I raised the barrel of the gun as high as I could over my head and brought it down with a striking blow. I heard a thud and continued to raise it again and again, repeatedly striking the crown of his head. The only thing I could think of was that I needed to render him unconscious and give myself enough time to escape.

Before I could raise the gun a fourth time, he violently grabbed my wrist and ripped the weapon from my hand. Once again the tables turned, and I was on the receiving end of the forceful blows. One after another, waves of nausea crashed over me. My body felt cold and numb, and I feared these waves would eventually take me under.

I told myself, *This can't be real. This must be a bad dream I will wake from at any moment.*

But I didn't wake up, and it wasn't a dream. I was trapped. This was really happening.

My thoughts snapped back to the present, and I could feel the closeness of my ex-husband's face as the distance between us narrowed. The repulsive stench of alcohol on his breath made my stomach churn, threatening to make me sick.

"If I really wanted to kill you, I could!" his words mocked. He aimed a gun at my bedroom wall. I held my breath and time stood still. I watched as he pulled the trigger. Closing my eyes, I braced with foreboding apprehension.

Kaboom!

The deafening sound reverberated in my ears. A hole the size of a half-dollar stared back at me from the once smooth sheetrock.

Kaboom!

The silence was broken again, leaving a hole just a little lower than the first.

Kaboom!

One final time he aimed the gun and fired, its deafening blast echoing through the room. The bullet tore into the wall just inches from where I stood. If I'd had any doubt before, it was gone. Not only was my ex-husband serious—he was also more dangerous than I could have ever imagined in my wildest dreams.

The next several hours blurred together. All sense of time seemed suspended. My body was beaten and abused in cruel ways, and I eventually wound up on my bed, broken and compromised. I clung to the hope that somehow, some way, I would still make it out of this alive. As reality seemed to distort around me, everything inside me screamed, "Hold on and fight!"

Suddenly, the air in my bedroom became very still and something strange happened. Amid the chaos all around me, I became aware of another presence in the room. I couldn't see this presence, yet somehow it felt oddly reassuring and familiar.

Could this be the presence of God?

The presence felt calm and peaceful. There also seemed to be a deep sense of sadness about it.

Had this presence been there with me the whole time? Had it silently witnessed the horrific events I had experienced over the last several hours?

I grappled with these questions until a realization dawned on me—this whole time I had never really been all alone!

I hadn't been alone in my pain. I hadn't been alone in my fear. I hadn't been alone in my suffering. I hadn't been alone in my sadness. Suddenly, I knew that this presence surrounding me must be the presence of God. Not only had He been there right beside me the whole time, but He was not about to walk out or leave me alone now. My heart knew that no matter what was about to happen, I was going to be okay.

In that moment, Psalm 23, which I had recited countless times as a child, echoed in my mind: "Yea though I walk through the valley of the shadow of death, I will fear no evil, for thou art with me." This familiar verse became more than just words; it became a tangible reality. Even though I knew I might be very close to death, a profound sense of peace washed over me, erasing all fear. I found comfort in the assurance that even in the darkest times, my heavenly Father remained by my side. His unwavering presence reassured me that I was not alone, even in my deepest fear, evoking the childlike faith I had known as a young girl.

> No matter the circumstances we go through in this life, God promises to walk alongside us and never leave us to face them alone.

God's presence and answers to our prayers come in many different ways and forms. Sometimes we get the exact answer we've been praying for. Other times God answers in a different way. Lying on my bed that day, I had peace knowing that whether God stopped it all or if I died and He ushered me home, I was going to be okay. Ultimately, this is what we all need to know. No matter the circumstances we go through in this life, God promises to walk alongside us and never leave us to face them alone.

Where Is God When Bad Things Happen?

As a therapist, I frequently encounter clients grappling with profound questions about the presence of adversity in their lives. They often ask, "Why did God allow this bad thing to happen?" I witness their struggle with questions like "Is God punishing me?" "Is He somehow trying to teach me a lesson?" "What did I do wrong?" "Why, if God is all-powerful, didn't He step in and stop it?"

In my candid response to these questions, I often begin by saying, "I don't have all the answers," a statement steeped in humility and the recognition that our human understanding is limited. Perhaps therein lies the essence of faith. If we understood everything or had all the answers, we wouldn't need faith or have to rely on God to be our answer. Faith is more than just a feeling. It is a deliberate choice to believe, even when we don't understand.

I remember when my four children were little. They often asked questions like "Why is the sky blue?" or "Why did God make bees?" Despite my best efforts to provide satisfactory explanations, my answers never quite seemed to satisfy their curiosity. No matter how hard I tried to get them to understand, their little minds couldn't grasp the enormity of my answers. They continued to ask, "But why?" until finally, recognizing that no answer I could offer was going to be good enough, I would say, "Just because."

You and I are God's children. When our human minds don't understand something, we keep asking Him, "But why?" Unlike my frustration at my children's repeated questions, God is patient with us. Our questions don't upset Him. He understands our need to try and make sense of things our human minds can't understand.

The book of Psalms is full of David's honest laments as he pours out his heart to the Lord. We see him continually bringing his questions to God: *Where are you? Why have you forsaken me? Why do you ignore my cries for help? How long must I struggle? Why do you feel so distant?*

What David does next, though, is vital: He follows his questions and complaints about how he *feels* with reminders and declarations of what he *knows* to be true about God's character. In Psalm 22, right after telling God he feels forsaken and ignored, David declares:

> Yet you are holy,
>> enthroned on the praises of Israel.
> Our ancestors trusted in you,
>> and you rescued them.
> They cried out to you and were saved.
>> They trusted in you and were never disgraced.
> (vv. 3–5 NLT)

In verses 23–24, he goes on to say:

> Praise the LORD, all you who fear him!
>   Honor him, all you descendants of Jacob!
>   Show him reverence, all you descendants of Israel!
> For he has not ignored or belittled the suffering of the
>   needy.
> He has not turned his back on them,
>   but has listened to their cries for help. (NLT)

Here is the takeaway: Bringing our frustrations to Jesus is not wrong. He welcomes our questions and complex emotions. It isn't sinful to ask Him, "Why?" Even Jesus, God's perfect Son, asked the Father, "Why have you forsaken me?"

Just because we ask "Why?" doesn't mean we will get the answers we're searching for. In our most significant moments of discouragement, we need to rehearse what we know to be true about the character of God. Exodus 34:6 tells us that God is compassionate and gracious, slow to anger and abounding in love and faithfulness. More than anything, God promises that He never changes. He is the same yesterday, today, and forever (Heb. 13:8).

In This World, You Will Have Trouble

So many Christians have been taught that if we live a righteous life and do the things God has asked us to do, everything should come easy. We've bought into the idea that as God's children we should hop, skip, and jump from one blessing to another. While that would be wonderful, in John 16:33 Jesus tells us the exact opposite is true: "I have told you these things, so that in me you may have peace. In this world you will have trouble. But take heart! I have overcome the world." In Psalm 34:19 we read, "Many are the afflictions of the righteous, but the LORD delivers him out of them all" (NKJV).

Nowhere in the Bible does God promise a life without hardship. He does promise that He will be there right beside us when we go through hard times. He promises that He will not abandon us or let us go through trials alone. He promises to be close to the brokenhearted and to weep with those who weep.

Just like you, I have many more questions than answers. I don't understand why God allows all the suffering in the world. I don't understand why innocent children get abused or why some people are healed and others aren't. What I do know is that the Bible says we live in a broken and fallen world. When Adam and Eve disobeyed God in the garden of Eden, sin entered this world, and Satan began roaming about, seeking whom he could destroy. I also know there are some things we will just never understand this side of eternity no matter how much we want to or how often we ask.

Discovering the Presence of God

Have you ever wondered, "Where was God in this situation?" We get our minds set on what we think God "should" do. We have expectations of what we think it would look like if He "showed up" on the scene. Too often we fail to recognize that just because we haven't seen God with our physical eyes, it doesn't mean that He was absent. If we stop and look closely, we will realize that we have seen God repeatedly. We have seen Him in the people He has brought across our path. We have seen Him in the opportunities and favor He has given us. And we have seen Him in His hand of provision and protection over our lives.

Genesis 28:11–16 takes on a new meaning when we read it in this light. In this passage, Jacob finds a stone to rest his head on and goes to sleep. In his dream, he sees a staircase that reaches from earth to heaven with angels going up and down it. At the top of the staircase is the Lord, who speaks a blessing on Jacob. In the morning, Jacob wakes and declares, "Surely the Lord is in this place, and I wasn't even aware of it!" (NLT).

How often has the Lord been in our midst and we haven't even been aware of it? He has been there in a precious friend's soft, warm embrace. He has been there in an encouraging word from a random stranger. And He has been there in the peace of His presence when nothing else seemed to make any sense. Our ability to see God is not limited to our physical sight.

Our ability to see God is not limited to our physical sight.

The morning my ex-husband held me against my will, I knew God was with me even if I could not see Him with my eyes. I knew He was standing right there beside me.

Into the Valley

The torture continued for several hours. By 4:30 a.m. I could tell the effects of alcohol were wearing off for my ex-husband, and I was unsure what he planned to do next. All he told me was that the night was not going to end well.

"I'm going to let you live, but you are going to be punished for ruining my life!" he shouted. "You didn't know it, but I've been following you. I've seen how much time you've spent with *that* man! I saw you go to his house last night. You're lucky you were gone when I drove back by his house two hours later. If you had still been there, I was going to come in and kill you both."

I couldn't believe what I was hearing.

"Get your clothes on!" he ordered. "It's time to finish the job I started. As part of your punishment, you're going to watch me kill your new boyfriend."

My heart raced and threatened to leap out of my chest at any moment. My hands clung to the banister in the long stairwell leading to the front door of my home. He followed just a few steps behind me as we descended the stairs. When we reached the tile entryway, one look outside confirmed that the truck he had arrived in was waiting.

The only thing I could think of was how I needed to stall. I needed to buy as much extra time as I could so Andrew would leave for work before we arrived at his home. Somehow, I needed to warn him.

My ex-husband forced me into his truck and then pulled out of the driveway. The truck accelerated and gained momentum. I watched the numbers on the speedometer climb as we drove in the direction of Andrew's home. I knew I was running out of time and frantically wondered how to escape. It seemed my only option would be to wait for a car to pull up behind us and then jump from the moving vehicle. If I timed it right, maybe I could find some cover and make my way to safety. All I had to do now was wait for just the right moment.

As I held my breath, I looked for any opportunity to jump out and run for help. I prayed he wouldn't notice me inching my fingers slowly toward the passenger door handle. The pounding in my chest got harder, and all I could feel was my mounting anticipation. My eyes were glued to the side passenger mirror as I watched for any sign of an approaching vehicle.

Ten minutes passed with no cars in sight. With each passing mile, my heart sank, knowing there was nothing left I could do. Nothing, that is, except quietly pray for the protection of the man my ex-husband was on his way to kill. The same man my heart had come to love.

I heard the gravel crunch as we pulled into Andrew's driveway. With one last look in my direction, my ex-husband reached into the back seat for a second gun. The front pocket of his wrinkled blue shirt bulged from the extra bullets he had stored there. Before exiting the truck, I heard him say, "Now you can go do whatever you need to do."

Horrified, I watched the few seconds it took for him to mount the three uneven cement steps leading to Andrew's front door. Taking a few steps backward, he gathered momentum and lunged forward to gain entry. When the solid wood door refused to budge, he aimed the gun at its leaded glass window.

Kaboom!

Kaboom!

Kaboom!

The shots rang out in quick succession, shattering the window. My heart sank; I knew it was over. I knew Andrew would have been on his way to the door after hearing all the commotion. Standing on the other side of it, he would have been shot multiple times. There was no way Andrew could have survived.

Adrenaline pulsed through my veins when I spotted the truck keys dangling from the ignition. I had to act fast. This was my chance to escape. And if I was wrong about what had just happened, if there was even the slightest chance Andrew could have survived, it was up to me to find help.

Wasting no time, I lunged into the driver's seat and slammed the truck into reverse. I held on tight and drove over the curbs. My body jolted from the impact as I navigated through the neighborhood in a frantic search for help. With each turn, my mind raced, oblivious to the distance I had covered from Andrew's house.

Finally, a 24-hour supermarket caught my attention. I plowed into the parking lot, leaped out of the vehicle, and sprinted toward the entrance. As the automatic doors slid open, I let out a piercing scream.

"911! Call 911!" I pleaded to the row of checkout cashiers dutifully tending their posts. "Somebody PLEASE call 911!" I begged. I was gasping for air, and my desperation grew when I realized no one was moving into action. Stunned faces just stared back at me. No one seemed to know what to do.

With mounting frustration, I screamed again. This time, my legs buckled beneath me. I didn't know what else I could do until I felt a hard object in my hand. Looking down, I realized in fear and confusion, I had grabbed my ex-husband's cell phone instead of my own. I prayed the phone would unlock if I dialed 911 and I'd finally be able to reach out for help.

"This is 911. What is your emergency?" I heard the voice on the other end of the line say.

"Please, oh please, send help!" I cried. "My ex-husband has a gun, and I think he's killed a man."

I told them the location and begged for someone to help.

"Don't worry, ma'am. Help is on the way," the operator said. "Stay on the line with me. Police are on the way."

"Please tell them to be careful!" I warned. "He said he will kill anyone who tries to stand in his way!"

Having done everything I could, I realized the situation was now out of my hands. Every emotion I had tried so hard to contain refused to be kept in any longer. My strength was gone and my body collapsed. Sobbing, I dropped to a heap on the floor.

By now it was seven o'clock and the early morning shoppers had made their way into the store. Though they tried to be courteous, there was no hiding the looks of horror on their faces. All at once, I became aware that every eye was focused on me.

"Follow me," a store clerk whispered. She removed her jacket and wrapped the long sleeves around my bruised and bloodied body. Ushering me to the safety of a back storeroom, her protective arm served as a shield from the onlookers' stares.

"You'll be safe here," she reassured me. Once again I crumpled into a heap on the floor. The meaning of her words pierced through my numb body. Finally, it dawned on me that my ex-husband would no longer be able to harm me.

One by one, store employees came to offer their comfort. I asked to borrow a cell phone and apprehensively dialed my parents' phone number, unsure if what my ex-husband had said about them being dead was true. I cried with relief when my mother answered the phone, unaware of what had happened. My mind quickly shifted to Andrew. Had he made it out alive? Fear gripped me. How could anyone have survived what had happened at his front door?

Twenty minutes passed before a police officer entered the storeroom and informed me an ambulance was there to take me to a nearby hospital.

"Follow me, ma'am," he said. "My partners and I will ensure you get out of here safely."

My insides were shaking, but I attempted a smile and politely thanked the store employees who had never left my side. Not wanting to draw additional attention to myself, I bowed my head low and focused on the floor as I made the long trek to the front door.

"Can I stop at the truck and get my cell phone?" I asked the officer who escorted me. It was important that I be the one to tell my children what happened. There was no way I wanted them to learn about the morning's events from a local news story.

The officer nodded his agreement and paused by the truck bed to wait for me. No one could have predicted what happened next. When I opened the passenger door, my ex-husband's face peered back at me from behind the steering wheel. Once again, a gun was aimed in my direction.

I would later learn that in my frantic state, I had repeatedly circled the same six-block area. Meanwhile, my ex-husband had left the scene on foot and happened upon his truck there in the supermarket parking lot. In my haste, I had left the truck unlocked, and before the police arrived on the scene he seized the opportunity to climb in and wait for my return.

My blood-curdling scream got the attention of police officers, who instinctually ran to form a human shield around me. While some of them surrounded the truck, others ushered me behind a large stone column at the store's entrance. Once again, the officer who had originally escorted me to safety promised he would stay by my side.

By now, what little strength I had left was gone. I didn't want to see or hear or feel anything else. So I stuck my fingers in my ears, closed my eyes tight, and silently began to pray. I prayed for the police officers who had donned bulletproof vests and were putting their lives in danger. I prayed that God would keep each one of the officers safe.

What took only minutes felt like an eternity as the police apprehended my ex-husband. Once he was in custody, the first responders placed me on a gurney and loaded me into an ambulance that whisked me to a nearby hospital where the ER staff was expecting me.

When I arrived at the hospital, the nurses transferred me to a bed, and a sterile, white curtain was pulled around me. I answered question after question from nurses, doctors, X-ray technicians, and detectives. As soon as my parents learned what happened to me, they rushed to be by my side. I knew I was out of danger, but one question still plagued me: *What had happened to Andrew?*

In the agonizing hours that followed, I received word that Andrew had survived but was in critical condition. However, due to the circumstances surrounding the incident, authorities remained tight-lipped as to his whereabouts. As a whirlwind of emotions swept through me, I longed for the comfort and refuge of my own home.

Home.

Where was home now? Where would I go? The house where I had spent the last thirteen years of my life and the place where I had raised my children now resembled nothing more than a prison. I knew there was no way this house would ever be my home again.

He Gives and Takes Away

While the details of our stories may be quite different, all stories of pain and betrayal, fear and loss, heartache and suffering have commonalities. At one time or another, we all find ourselves in a place where it feels like our world has fallen apart. There are circumstances that we have little to no control over, and life knocks us off our feet.

I recently read a blog post by the late Jane Marczewski, a singer who performed under the stage name Nightbirde. Before the age of thirty, she was diagnosed with terminal cancer. Shortly after her diagnosis, doctors gave her six months to live and a two percent chance of survival. If that wasn't enough, her husband told her he no longer loved her, and her marriage ended in divorce. In her blog, Nightbirde wrote,

> I haven't come as far as I'd like in understanding the things that have happened this year. But here's one thing I do know; when it comes to pain, God isn't often in the business of taking it away. Instead, he adds to it. He is more of a giver than a taker. He doesn't take away my darkness, he adds light. He doesn't spare me of thirst, he brings water. He doesn't cure my loneliness, he comes near. So why do we believe that when we are in pain, it must mean God is far?[1]

Her words resonated with me. It was at the height and depth of my own pain that I felt God's presence closer than ever before. My sweet friend, I pray that as you hold and read this book, you feel Jesus standing close beside you. You may not physically see Him with your eyes, you may not physically hear Him with your ears, but I pray you physically sense Him like a warm blanket that envelops you and holds you close. How I wish I were there to put my arms around you and say, "I understand. I've got you." But more importantly, God promises that He's got you! In Deuteronomy 31:8 we read, "Do not be afraid or discouraged, for the LORD will personally go ahead of you. He will be with you; he will neither fail you nor abandon you" (NLT).

I pray that today you let yourself be held in the arms of God's never-ending grace and comfort.

PAUSE AND REFLECT

- Think of times when you couldn't physically see God but knew He was there and felt His presence. Take a moment to reflect on this and thank Him.

- Are there questions you have repeatedly asked God and still don't have answers to? Write those questions down and surrender them to God. Ask Him to help you trust Him even when you don't understand.

- Reflect on the times God has used other people to love you when you needed it most. Consider sending them a note of appreciation. Make a list of ways you can be Jesus's hands and feet to bless others. This might look like offering a word of encouragement, taking time to visit someone God places on your heart, or stopping for a few moments to pray for someone.

- During times of crisis, seeking support from licensed professionals trained in trauma healing can be immensely beneficial. Christian mental health professionals, in particular, offer a unique perspective that integrates faith into the healing process. They can provide specialized guidance and therapeutic interventions to help individuals navigate through their pain and move toward healing. Don't hesitate to reach out for professional help to ensure you receive the support and resources needed to overcome the challenges you're facing. (See "The Power of Therapy" in the Tools for Growth and Healing.)

PRAYER OF OUR HEART

Father, thank You for the times You found a way to show Your love for me—even when I didn't see You. For the friends You sent my way, the kind words I received from a stranger, and the unexpected blessings I forgot to give You credit for,

I thank You. Thank You for loving me at my lowest. For loving me when all I could see was my pain. Forgive me for the times I doubted Your love for me and for the times I may have stopped believing in You. Thank You, heavenly Father, for never giving up on me! Amen.

6

A TIME TO HEAL

Moving from "Why Me?" to "What Now?"

It is in the storms that God does His finest work, for it is in the storms that God has our keenest attention.

MAX LUCADO

He has sent me to bind up the brokenhearted, . . .
to bestow on them a crown of beauty
    instead of ashes,
the oil of joy
    instead of mourning,
and a garment of praise
    instead of a spirit of despair.

ISAIAH 61:1–3

It had been a grueling day, one that stretched on endlessly. Not only had I been answering what seemed to be the same questions over and over, but I had also endured one exam after another. Amid the chaos of the morning, the wound on the top of my head had been stapled shut, X-rays had been taken to ensure there were no broken bones, and my abrasions had been carefully cleansed.

When the questions and exams were finally complete, a nurse directed me to the shower and laid out a clean pair of ill-fitting clothes for me to wear home. I was told the ones I had entered the hospital with were now considered evidence and had to be left behind. The clothes I was given had been taken from the hospital donation box and felt like a metaphor for the uncertain path that lay ahead of me. Trying to rebuild a life once full of dreams was like fitting together scattered pieces of a puzzle that needed to be put back together again.

My body was aching. Mom and I slowly walked to the hospital parking lot and got into her car. At her insistence, I agreed to stay with her and my dad for a while. She understood there was no way I would want to return to my home—the place where less than twelve hours earlier my entire life had changed forever. I knew I would eventually need to plan my next steps. For now, all I could think of was how desperately I wanted to sleep and be in the safety of my parents' home.

I use the word "safety," but in all honesty, nothing could have been further from the truth. All sense of safety was gone. For the first time in my life, I felt broken. Additionally, I couldn't shake the worry that somehow my ex-husband would get out of jail and come after me, leaving me in constant fear and anxiety.

Before that day, I had never liked to use the word "broken" when referring to people who have experienced some form of trauma. When I got my first job as a therapist, I worked for a small non-profit agency. Our main clientele was families who had experienced child abuse or neglect, and it was not uncommon to hear people refer to children from these homes as broken.

Something about this word never sat well with me. In my mind, when something was broken, it was damaged beyond repair. It meant there was no value left, and the only thing to do was throw it away. Because of this, I often corrected anyone who used this word and asked them to replace it with the word "wounded." But when I left the hospital emergency room that day following my attack, I finally understood what it meant to truly feel broken.

That night, when it was time to go to bed, I reluctantly asked my grown daughters, who had come to stay with me, to sleep next to me. I insisted we keep a small light on just in case I needed to find my way to the bathroom. In reality, it was not a fear of the dark but rather the darkness of fear that surrounded me. A fear that kept me awake, bracing time and time again, waiting for the moment my bedroom door might come crashing down around me again.

My daughters sensed my fear that night because each silently reached for my hand. They lay as close to me as they could for reassurance. Then, with a quiet voice, I heard my youngest daughter begin to pray.

"Lord, we ask that You hold all our hearts tonight. Thank You that You are so good! Even though bad things have happened today, You alone are good!" Years later, I learned that in those first few nights, my youngest daughter arranged for the police to do nightly drive-bys and patrol my parents' home, making sure that all of us were safe.

The following days were long and hard as they moved forward one painful moment at a time. The bruises on my body began to fade, but the bruises on my heart and mind only continued to grow deeper. My heart sank when Andrew's children, only one of whom I had met, reached out to offer their best wishes along with the suggestion that we should both move forward in separate directions. This only heightened my sense of unease and added to the mounting concern weighing heavily on my shoulders.

It was the end of the first week when my uncle and aunt unexpectedly stopped by for a visit. I watched their eyes brim with tears at the sight of bruises framing my swollen eyes. My uncle came near and gently put his arm around my shoulder, careful not to hurt my aching body. He asked if we could go somewhere private to talk.

"Kim, your aunt and I are leaving for the summer," he said. "We've thought long and hard and would like to offer you the use of our home while we're gone. If you want it, it's yours for the asking. Drop by our house, and we'll show you where to find everything."

I was grateful for the offer. After the assault, my sense of security had shattered. Even with my ex-husband in jail, I couldn't shake off the feeling of being vulnerable. My uncle and aunt's home, located near my parents, provided a haven where I could begin to rebuild. The fact that only my family would know my whereabouts added an extra layer of comfort and safety.

I knew the plan he suggested was only temporary. Mostly, I just wanted things to get back to some semblance of normalcy. I felt certain I'd never feel safe going back to my old place, so despite lacking a long-term plan, I accepted their offer, eager for the security it promised.

When I arrived at their home the next day, my uncle and aunt told me to consider this house as my own for the next five months. They said there was plenty of room for my children, who would also be welcome here. This was a comfort to me, as it was nearing summer break and my youngest children would be coming to stay with me.

When I followed my uncle and aunt into their large, private backyard, I saw, tucked among a group of trees, a beautiful pergola with two weathered swings. Its cement patio floor was large enough it could have been a stage. Gazing at it in awe, I knew in my heart this was the place I was going to meet Jesus.

Standing on Holy Ground

In Exodus 3, Moses had an encounter with God. He'd been shepherding his father-in-law's sheep near Mount Horeb, also called the mountain of God. While there, he saw a bush on fire, but it wasn't consumed by the flames. When Moses went in for a closer look, God's voice called his name from out of the burning bush and instructed him to take off his sandals. God then told Moses, "the place where you are standing is holy ground" (v. 5).

As I stood before my uncle and aunt's beautiful pergola, I knew this too was a holy place where I would encounter a holy God. I felt drawn to this spot with expectation. I sensed that God not only knew me but was waiting for me. I felt God calling out my name just as He did with Moses.

On my first day at my uncle and aunt's house, I donned a bathrobe and wrapped myself as tightly as possible in a thick green blanket borrowed from a nearby couch. The patio door easily slid open beneath my touch, and I placed my cup of coffee on a table just outside. The sun peeked through the leaves and offered my body some much-needed warmth. I was still sore, and my head throbbed with pain from hours of crying myself to sleep the night before.

My bare feet took me toward the center of the patio, where trees canopied the pergola. I slowly knelt and allowed myself to cry. It didn't take long before my tears turned to sobs that racked my exhausted body. No longer able to remain in an upright position, I lay prostrate and pressed my face against the cold cement.

This became my daily ritual during my first week at the pergola. Hour upon hour, my whole body wailed with sounds from deep within. My words were few, but my cries were long and hard.

Grief Is Healthy, Grief Is Hard, Grief Is Holy

Did you know that God gave us grief as a gift? Grief allows us to express sorrow when we lose something or someone that deeply matters to us. It allows us to express the hurt we feel inside that we were wronged by circumstances beyond our control.

Don't get me wrong. Grief doesn't feel good, and in the moment it might feel like anything but a gift. That's likely why we often try so hard to avoid it or distract ourselves from it. We attempt to push it aside, to stay busy, or to escape reminders of the pain. But something I've learned is that grief refuses to be silenced. It inevitably finds a way to the surface, demanding to be acknowledged and felt.

Grief and sorrow are similar feelings, but they have their own meanings. Sorrow is like a deep sadness we feel when something or someone important to us is lost. It's the sadness we feel because of something bad that happened. Grief is a bigger feeling caused by loss. It includes sadness as well as other feelings like emptiness and confusion, and it can even manifest physically. Grief is a process of dealing with loss, and it's not just about feeling sad. It's about adjusting to life after something important is gone. So, while sorrow is part of grief, grief itself is a bigger and longer-lasting response to loss.

> Grief refuses to be silenced. It inevitably finds a way to the surface, demanding to be acknowledged and felt.

In her article "The Gift of Grief," Kellie Johnson writes, "Grief is too powerful an emotion to be left alone. It cries out for attention, and if we keep it at bay too long, it will soak into us like a sponge, bringing a heaviness into our spirit and causing us to be ineffective and unproductive in our daily activities. It will affect our hearts and relationships and distract us from our daily lives."[1] God created all our emotions and intends them to be expressed in healthy ways for us to process life's ups and downs. When it comes to grief, it's like having a dishwasher for our emotions. Just like a dishwasher goes through cycles to clean dishes, our grief also has its own cycles. It includes stages like sadness, anger, and acceptance. If we keep interrupting this cycle, it's like stopping the dishwasher before it finishes cleaning. Our grief doesn't get fully processed, and we can't move forward. Allowing ourselves to go through the whole cycle of grief is important for healing and moving on.

So, how does one move forward and begin to heal? This may look different for each of us. For some it means crying until there are no tears left. For others, it involves journaling intimate feelings and prayers to God. Still others might find a quiet place to reflect and remember. And some people benefit from verbally processing out loud with a friend or paid professional. If you're anything like me, expressing grief might combine all of these.

Give Yourself Space to Grieve

Years ago, I visited Vancouver, British Columbia. It was the rainy season, and I marveled at how everyone refused to let rain interfere with their plans. Most people carried an umbrella wherever they went, ensuring they'd always be ready. Whether a light sprinkle, a steady rain, or even a downpour, they were always prepared for whatever came their way.

This is much the same with grief. Grief is unpredictable and can show up as a sprinkle, a steady rain, or a downpour of emotions when you least expect it. By allowing yourself the space and time to feel grief, you acknowledge that your season of sadness will eventually evolve into a beautiful new season—but not before you are ready.

Grief often leaves us feeling isolated and alone in our pain. In those moments, it is important to remember that we are not grieving alone. In Psalm 34:18, God's Word promises, "The LORD is close to the brokenhearted and saves those who are crushed in spirit." We need to gently remind ourselves that God's love is greater than our pain, and He stays with us through it all.

Be Honest with God About How You Feel

When we deny our feelings, we only stay stuck in our pain. God already knows what we are feeling, so nothing is gained when we try to disguise them. Romans 8:38–39 puts it this way:

> And I am convinced that nothing can ever separate us from God's love. Neither death nor life, neither angels nor demons, neither our fears for today nor our worries about tomorrow—not even the powers of hell can separate us from God's love. No power in the sky above or in the earth below—indeed, nothing in all creation will ever be able to separate us from the love of God that is revealed in Christ Jesus our Lord. (NLT)

That means our feelings of sadness, disappointment, frustration, and anger will never change God's love for us. Let me say that again: God's love for us will never change! God wants us to acknowledge our feelings and be honest with Him.

Time and time again, I stood beneath the pergola, crying out to God and telling Him I didn't understand His plan. I told Him I felt He had abandoned me. I told Him I felt He had let me down. I told Him how scared I was to trust Him with my heart again.

And then I told Him I loved Him.

I am reminded of a time when my son was five years old. I had just dropped him and his sisters off at school. It was our daily practice that each time he exited our minivan, he'd stop to smile at me and hold his little fingers up in the sign for "I love you." My response was always to return the sign while mouthing the words "I love you too!"

On this particular day, my son was angry with me about something. When it came time to drop him off at school, there was no backward glance or signed "I love you." Instead, he stiffly held his arm next to his side. Though he was mad at me and tried to distance himself and push me away, my mama heart only wanted to run after him, scoop him up in my arms, and reassure him of my love. I wasn't angry that he was angry at me. The opposite was true. My heart was saddened by the emotional distance my son was trying to put in place due to his anger with me.

> God's steadfast love for you and me is never-ending, never-changing, and never-failing.

Just as I continued to love my son even though he was mad at me, God loves us even when we are angry. He understands our hurt, anger, and disappointment. When we feel like pushing Him away, He is right there beside us and wants nothing more than to scoop us up in His arms. That's how big His love is! God's steadfast love for you and me is never-ending, never-changing, and never-failing.

Choose to Guard Your Heart

When we suppress our emotions and fail to acknowledge them in healthy ways, we run the risk of getting stuck and becoming captive to our circumstances. The Bible tells the story of a woman who did just that.

The book of Ruth opens in chapter 1 with a man named Elimelech and his wife, Naomi. They take their two sons and leave their hometown of Bethlehem in Judah because of a famine in the land. When they arrive in the country of Moab, Elimelech and Naomi decide to settle there. But Elimelech dies, and Naomi is left as a single mother raising her two sons.

Years go by, and Naomi's sons grow up and marry Moabite women. Not long after this, both of Naomi's sons die, and she is left with her two daughters-in-law, Ruth and Orpah. Not knowing what else to do, Naomi decides to return to her homeland of Judah, and she encourages her daughters-in-law to return to their mothers' homes. Orpah agrees, but Ruth refuses to leave Naomi's side, and together they journey back to Bethlehem.

When Naomi and Ruth finally arrive in Bethlehem, they are greeted with enthusiasm by the local women who ask, "Can this be Naomi?"

Now, this is where the story takes a turn.

When the women of Bethlehem show their excitement in welcoming Naomi home, Naomi makes a declaration: "Don't call me Naomi; call me Bitter. The Strong One has dealt me a bitter blow. I left here full of life, and GOD has brought me back with nothing but the clothes on my back. Why would you call me Naomi? God certainly doesn't. The Strong One ruined me" (1:20 MSG).

Notice that God did not change Naomi's name. It was Naomi herself who changed it. Life had not been fair to her, so she declared, "From now on, I will be known as Bitter."

Naomi *chose* to become bitter.

Like Naomi, have you fallen into hard circumstances that you didn't see coming your way? Have others made choices that you have been forced to pay the price for? Have you lost a spouse or child to death? Has someone turned on you and betrayed the trust you placed in them? Have you been wrongfully accused by others or had rumors spread about you? Has sickness hit you or your family? What in life has been unfair to you? How have you responded? Have you allowed yourself to drown in anger or bitterness, refusing to let yourself move forward? Have you become stuck in your pain? Like Naomi, we all have a choice in how we will respond to the unfairness that life so often brings our way.

We may have had *no choice* in what happened to us, but we have *every choice* in how we are going to respond.

Weeks after the attack, one of my daughters came to me and asked if I remembered what I had said to her when she visited me in the emergency room. I thought momentarily, then confessed I had not remembered much from that day. My daughter smiled and said, "Mom, you said, 'Please promise me you won't let this make you bitter.'"

A few months later, I ran into the police detective assigned to my case. She asked me if I remembered what I had said to her the day we met for the first time in the emergency room. Once again, I replied that I only remembered a little from that day. The detective reminded me, "Kim, you told me you would not let this experience go to waste. You said you would become a better therapist because of it."

> We may have had **no choice** in what happened to us, but we have **every choice** in how we are going to respond.

I don't tell you about these responses to glorify myself or to imply that I am anything special. I also don't want you to think that I wasn't hurting on the inside, because I was. The reason I share these responses is that for the past seventeen years as a therapist, I have witnessed firsthand the effects unforgiveness and bitterness have had on people when they are hit by some of life's most brutal pain. The responses I gave in the hospital emergency room on the day of my attack weren't based on my feelings. Instead, I was making a declaration that had nothing to do with my feelings. I was declaring that I would go through the process of healing and not allow my hurt to keep me stuck.

The legal process continued for several months, causing me to make repeated trips to the district attorney's office. Each time I arrived, I was required to check in at the front desk, where I was asked to sign my name. The first time I did this, I hesitated when

I saw an arrow indicating where I was expected to sign. The red arrow pointed to a column labeled "Victim Sign Here."

Something inside me bristled, and I resisted signing my name. I didn't want to be known or identified as a "victim." My name was Kim, and I wanted everyone to understand that while I had been *victimized* and something terrible had happened *to* me, that was not who I was and that was not who I would allow myself to become. I knew I had a choice to make. Like Naomi, I could change my name to "bitter" and let what had happened to me define me. Or I could choose to do the emotional work required to come out of this victorious.

Today, wherever you are as you read this, I want to speak a truth into your heart: Whatever darkness you may be facing, there's a light waiting to break through. What others intended for evil in our lives, God not only *can* but *will* redeem for good (Gen. 50:20).

Don't shy away from the pain. Lean into it. It's okay to feel hurt, sadness, and even anger. These emotions are part of our journey, and it is crucial to acknowledge them and navigate through them in healthy ways. But don't get stuck in your pain.

Refuse to let the enemy have the final say in your life. We are daughters of the Most High God, loved beyond measure and cherished beyond comprehension. Today, let's choose to stand firm in the truth of who we are and believe what God has spoken and declared over us as His precious children. We can walk forward with courage, knowing that God is faithful in redeeming every broken piece of our lives.

Guard Your Mind: Winning the War Through Worship

In 2 Corinthians 10:4–5, Paul tells us, "The weapons we fight with are not the weapons of the world. On the contrary, they have divine power to demolish strongholds. We demolish arguments and every pretension that sets itself up against the knowledge of God, and we take captive every thought to make it obedient to Christ."

It took only a few days at the pergola before I realized that since the attack, my thoughts had been consumed by worries and were running rampant. I was struggling to keep my heart and mind focused on the promises of God, and I knew I needed to somehow guard what I was thinking. My moods were up and down, and I felt I had no control over them.

Feeling overwhelmed by my emotions and the situation, I sought solace in prayer. Tears streamed down my face as I poured out my heart to God, burdened by challenges that seemed impossible to overcome. I wasn't expecting an answer when I asked the Lord how I was going to make it through. But then something unexpected happened. In the midst of my tears, a quiet voice stirred deep within me, whispering, "With a song!"

Those simple words sparked a flicker of hope within me. They reminded me of the solace I've always found in music, suggesting that perhaps a melody could guide me through this difficult time. And indeed, music would prove to be a beacon of light in the weeks and months ahead, helping me find my way through the storm.

When You Worship, Demons Flee

In 1 Samuel 16:14–23, we read how music played a crucial role in alleviating King Saul's troubles. When the Spirit of God departed from Saul, he became tormented by an evil spirit. The only thing that could settle him or bring him peace was when the shepherd boy David came and played his harp for him. "And whenever the tormenting spirit from God troubled Saul, David would play the harp. Then Saul would feel better, and the tormenting spirit would go away" (v. 23 NLT).

Here I stood under the pergola, overwhelmed with worry and an unsettled mind of my own. I knew that to win this battle, I needed to find a way to speak louder than the noisy feelings screaming inside me.

More than anything, I knew I needed God's help. I bowed on my knees and began to whisper a prayer based on Zephaniah 3:17.

"Father, please help me calm my fears. I am asking you to please sing your songs of deliverance over me."

I realized I needed to align my words and thoughts with the truths found in God's Word, especially those that applied to my situation. To combat the despair threatening to overwhelm me, I had to take action. For me, that meant engaging in a battle for my mind and heart. Singing worship songs became my weapon in this fight.

Worship Changes Your Focus and Puts It on God

Whenever we let our minds wander to worry, our focus turns to ourselves and the hard situations we are going through. When we *decide* to worship (yes, it is a choice!), our focus turns toward God and His greatness.

When I want to emphasize the power of our thoughts to my therapy clients, I often conduct a simple exercise. I ask them to scan my office and count all the blue items they see. They usually spot the blue curtains, pillows, and decor. Then I ask if they were thinking about my blue decor before our session, and they usually say no. When I ask why they noticed it now, they say it's because I asked them to count the items. I conclude by explaining that they noticed the blue items because they were actively seeking them out. This simple exercise reveals how our focus shapes our perception. The realization often dawns on them with profound clarity.

While we need to grieve, we can't stay focused on our problems. Focusing solely on our problems can be overwhelming. When we shift our focus to the goodness of God, our problems become smaller. The point is that you will find what you focus on.

Worship Builds Your Faith

It is up to us to build up our faith and encourage ourselves in the Lord. We do this by believing and consistently reminding ourselves of what the Word of God says. Hebrews 4:12–13 describes the Word of God as "alive and active" and "sharper than any double-edged sword." In Romans 10:17 Paul emphasizes that faith grows as we hear and absorb the Word of God.

As I sat on the swing that hung from the pergola rafters, I searched the music apps on my phone for lyrics that would encourage me. Song after song resonated deeply within me as I found myself meditating on the meaningful words being sung. These included declarations like "I Will Praise You in This Storm," "You're a Good, Good Father," "I Am Not Alone," "You Are with Me," "God Will Make a Way," and "Gentle Healer." The song "Glorious Ruins" particularly touched me. It talks about how God still reigns and can bring beauty out of the messiest parts of our lives, even when everything seems like it's falling apart.

Listening to this song took me back to the day after my divorce was finalized. I had cried myself to sleep the night before and had woken up feeling physically and emotionally drained. Just getting out of bed that morning seemed like a huge accomplishment. When I picked up my cell phone from the nightstand, I found a message from my nephew in California that brought tears to my eyes.

Aunt Kim, I can't really imagine your whirlwind of emotions. You've definitely been on my heart a lot lately. I visited a church recently where a guest minister spoke about Glorious Ruins. It was all about how God takes something the world sees as ruined and turns it into something glorious. Although your situation is seen as ruins by the world's standards, I truly believe God has and will use it to show you His glory through you. I love you![2]

Now, four years later, I faced another period of devastation. My life, once full of dreams and plans, lay in pieces around me. Like an ancient city ravaged by time, my world had crumbled, leaving behind a landscape of broken promises and shattered expectations.

The song's message challenged me to look beyond my current destruction. Could these "ruins" of my life really turn into something good? It seemed hard to believe, but a spark of hope flickered inside me. Even though things looked bad now, maybe there was still a chance for something new and better to come.

Your Time to Heal

Take a moment to reflect on your own life. Do you find yourself surrounded by what seem like endless ruins? Has life thrown you into chaos, leaving you feeling helpless and lost? Have things fallen apart, and no matter how hard you try, it seems there is no way out?

Oh sister, hold on and be encouraged! You see, what the world calls broken and beyond repair, God sees as promise and possibility. What seems impossible by natural means is God's starting point. Eric Liddell, a Scottish runner whose story of winning an Olympic gold medal was chronicled in the movie *Chariots of Fire*, writes, "Circumstances may appear to wreck our lives and God's plans, but God is not helpless among the ruins."[3]

God is not intimidated by the broken pieces of our lives; in fact, He specializes in turning brokenness into beauty. God is in the business of repairing, rebuilding, and restoring.

So take heart. Even in your darkest moments, remember that God is at work behind the scenes, weaving together a masterpiece of redemption and renewal. Cling to hope, for the ruins of today can become the foundation for a brighter tomorrow.

PAUSE AND REFLECT

- Do you have a special place or time that you deliberately set aside to be with the Lord? Any time or place becomes holy when you and He show up! If you don't already have this practice, find a place you can go where you can set the cares of the world aside. Make a conscious decision to keep these appointments with Jesus. (See "The Power of Place" in the Tools for Growth and Healing.)

- Consider the significance of honoring and making space for your grief. Acknowledge that grief is not a weakness but a testament to the depth of your love and loss. Embrace the truth that grief is both hard and holy work, essential for healing. Allow yourself to feel your emotions fully without rushing through them. By honoring your grief, you open the door to healing and transformation, finding strength and resilience along the way.

- While it's crucial to acknowledge and grieve our difficulties, dwelling on them endlessly only magnifies their impact. Make a practice of daily reflecting on what you are grateful for. It could be something as simple as the warmth of the sun on your face or the laughter of a loved one. Write it down or say it out loud to remind yourself of the blessings in your life. Over time, this practice can transform your outlook and bring greater emotional well-being. (See "The Power of Gratitude" in Tools for Growth and Healing.)

- Life can be hard and leave us reeling from situations beyond our control. It becomes easy to slip into self-pity and take on the label of "victim." One strategy to guard against this is to stop and pray and ask the Lord how He sees the situation. Ask Him how He sees you and what He would like you to know. Then get quiet. Listen for His nudging in your heart. If you don't hear anything, that's okay. God also speaks through His written Word. Write down whatever it is you feel you are hearing Him say.

- It is important to guard what we put into our minds. Consider making a playlist of songs to listen to when you need encouragement. (See "The Power of Music" in the Tools for Growth and Healing.)

————————— **PRAYER OF OUR HEART** —————————

Oh Jesus, here I am with my heart held up, and I am asking You to mend it. I ask You to forgive me for the times I have refused to let go of anger or bitterness. More than anything, I want the freedom that comes from surrendering my emotions to You. Help me become aware of the thoughts and words I allow in my life. Thank You for being bigger than any problems I am currently facing. Help me always to endeavor to see my situation through the eyes of faith. Lord, I declare that You are restoring me, redeeming what has been stolen from me, and reviving my love for You. In Jesus's name I pray. Amen.

7

A TIME TO TRUST

Letting God Lead and Choosing to Follow

Sweet Jesus, teach me to trust and put my total confidence in You.
Give me the faith of a little child.

FROM THE AUTHOR'S JOURNAL FIVE YEARS BEFORE HER ASSAULT

Trust GOD from the bottom of your heart;
don't try to figure out everything on your own.
Listen for GOD's voice in everything you do, everywhere
you go;
he's the one who will keep you on track.

PROVERBS 3:5–6 MSG

Two weeks passed, and I still hadn't heard from Andrew. Then I got an update from his assistant at work. Unfortunately, it was not the news my heart so badly wanted to hear. She told me that the day after the incident, Andrew had expressed his love for me but said he needed time to sort things out. However, within a few days, his feelings had changed, and he no longer wanted to see me. She also mentioned that due to the severity of his injuries, Andrew had taken medical leave from work indefinitely. He had moved in with his adult son, who was helping him recover.

How could this have happened? All my dreams for a wonderful future seemed to be slipping away. More than anything, I longed to know that things would work out okay.

As long as I can remember, I've wanted a promise or guarantee. At thirteen years old, I asked my dad to promise I would live until the rapture. When I was fresh out of high school, it seemed all my girlfriends had boyfriends or were getting married, and I asked my mom to promise me that someday I would marry too. When my infant son was born with a genetic disease and was in the hospital for testing, I cried and asked my older sister to promise me he was going to be okay. When my mom was diagnosed with breast cancer, I asked her to promise me she was going to live and not die.

Looking back, I see each of my requests for promises came from a place of worry and fear. I desperately wanted reassurance that everything and everyone who mattered to me would be all right. The thought of anything different caused me unbearable distress.

Here it was, years later, and once again, I found myself searching for a promise that everything was going to be okay. Everything seemed so unfair, and there was nothing I could do about it. So I did the only thing I knew to do: I took matters into my own hands.

I exhausted my list of friends, calling them all and asking for prayer. Not only did I ask them to pray, but I also told them exactly what they were to ask God for. I begged to be put on every prayer chain possible and then issued exact instructions for how to pray. My prayers rose from a place of panic and seemed more like marching orders for what I wanted God to do. I didn't just tell Him what I wanted; I also told Him how He should get it done.

My prayers sounded something like this:

Lord, I trust You with everything in me. I know Your Word says that You want to give Your children the desires of their hearts. Lord, I desire that You please put a Kim-shaped hole in Andrew's heart and make him want to come back to me. It would be an amazing testimony, and I would give You all the glory. Oh, and Lord . . . if You could make it happen this week, I'd appreciate it!

Without realizing it, I had unintentionally rewritten Jeremiah 29:11. My personal version sounded more like this:

For I know the plans I have for myself, says Kim. Plans to prosper me the way I would like so I don't have to endure any discomfort. Plans to get me what I want, when I want it, and how I want it. Plans to give me everything I hope for to get the exact future I want.

The problem with the Kim version of this verse is that I lost sight of the fact that God has a plan, and His plan was and is far bigger and better than anything I could ever dream for myself (Eph. 3:20). My lips were saying, "I trust you, God," but in all reality, I was making myself lord of my own life. I wanted to be the one in control.

Isn't that what we so often do? The times we feel the most powerless and out of control are the exact times we tend to fight the hardest for control. We tell God we trust Him and His plan for our lives, but then we treat Him like our personal genie in a bottle whose sole purpose is to grant our every wish. Adding insult to injury, we find a passage of Scripture, take it out of context, and then try to convince God this is what He's promised us.

Focusing our eyes on our circumstances causes our fears to overpower our faith. That's why it's so important to guard our minds. It is impossible for fear and faith to coexist. When we allow our fears to consume us, it becomes easy to hear and align ourselves with the devil's lies—the lies that say things like, "What if God doesn't come through for you this time?" "Things will only get worse!" "You missed your opportunity and life has passed you by!"

No Other Idols

In my desperate effort to remain in control, I contacted my pastor's wife, and she agreed to meet for coffee. I poured out my heart and tried to get her on board with how I thought she should pray. I told her how my thoughts of Andrew consumed me from the moment I woke each morning until I went to bed each night.

I didn't get very far before she reached across the table and gently put her hand on top of mine.

"Kim, you're making Andrew your idol and putting him in the place of God. Your joy can never be found in him. It can only be found in God."

As I sat across from my pastor's wife, sipping my coffee and trying to absorb her words, something inside me stirred. It was as if God Himself was speaking directly to my heart, urging me to confront my struggle with surrender. I recognized that even though I had been telling God I surrendered my plans to Him, the only one I had been fooling was myself. More than anything, my heart wanted to surrender control, but somehow my fear kept getting in the way.

Trusting in God's Leadership

In both my personal journey and my professional journey as a therapist, I've come to understand the importance of surrendering control to God's leadership. One example of this surrender is in a twelve-step recovery program, where the first step involves admitting powerlessness and recognizing the need for a higher power. Subsequent steps emphasize belief in a greater power and a decision to surrender one's life and will to God's care. This process isn't about rushing through but rather embracing a gradual, intentional surrender that allows God to guide us forward.

My life following the assault reinforced facts I already knew from helping clients in recovery. I was powerless and my life had become unmanageable. I also believed only God could restore my life to a place of sanity. But while I believed in God and His promises, I struggled when it came to turning my life and will over to His care. Sometimes it is easier to believe *in* something but much harder to follow through and *do* something. This was one of those times for me.

Questions kept running through my mind. *What if I turned my life over to God only to have everything blow up in my face? What if I surrendered my will but everything I wanted was taken away?* I knew this was going to be the hardest step of faith I had ever taken. It would mean I had to agree to let God be God and stop my attempts at trying to do things my own way.

I know I'm not alone in this type of struggle. Perhaps you, too, have a hard time letting go of control. If you're anything like me, one of the hardest things to do is trust someone other than yourself with your future—even God. We sing the words "All to Jesus I surrender, all to Him I freely give," but when it comes right down to it, we often selectively pick and choose which parts of our life we are willing to surrender, clinging to certain areas we'd rather control ourselves.

> Surrender becomes easier when we trust the person in charge.

Real surrender begins with a decision to give up control to God. This decision cannot be based on our feelings because, let's face it, our feelings are fickle and can change at a moment's notice. If we wait for the perfect time, we risk staying stuck in the same place and might never take that leap of faith.

But here's the thing: Surrender becomes easier when we trust the person in charge. It's also easier to trust the person in charge if it's someone we already know. And who better to trust than God? Trust doesn't just happen overnight though; it's cultivated over time.

Cultivating Trust

So, how do we learn to trust God? We spend time with Him. It's the same idea as when we make new friends and are getting to know them. Our friendships deepen as we spend time together. We get to know God by spending time reading His Word, talking to Him in prayer, becoming still enough to hear His voice, and honoring Him with our worship. When we make these our regular practice, we slowly but surely learn how to listen and discern the voice of God in our hearts.

Spending time with God is a privilege, something that we, as His children, *get to do*. He does not demand that we *have to* spend time with Him but offers an open invitation for us to get to know Him. And the more time we spend with Him, the more we will want to. The more we invest in this relationship, the more natural surrender becomes and the more our trust in Him deepens.

In the first few days following the attack, my prayers sounded much like the classic children's book *The Little Engine That*

Could—you know, that cute story where the little blue train keeps saying, "I think I can, I think I can, I think I can," as it chugs up a seemingly insurmountable mountain.[1] The little engine used positive self-talk to keep himself motivated. But I needed more than positive self-talk; I needed divine intervention. So, one day out at the pergola, I lifted my voice up in prayer.

"Lord, I want to trust You," I whispered. Then, with a little more boldness, I said, "Lord, I'm trying to trust You." Finally, with all the honesty I could muster, I said, "Lord, I'm scared to trust You. Please teach me to trust You!"

> **Faith is not about feelings. It's about deciding to trust in what you can't see or fully comprehend.**

It was a raw, honest moment. I poured out my heart to God as I wavered between fear and faith. I admitted my hesitancy to relinquish control and trust Him to lead and care for me. I told God how much I loved Him. However, my real struggle wasn't about my love for Him but whether I could trust Him with my life.

In the days after I prayed that prayer, it felt like my heart was in a constant tug-of-war. Whenever I focused on my circumstances, panic would start to set in. I'd cling to any glimmer of hope, wishing the outcome I desired. But then, when I turned my gaze to the Lord and the promises in His Word, peace would wash over me, reassuring me that I could trust Him with everything.

This battle went on for several weeks until one day I realized I had been treating my faith as if it were a feeling. If I felt confident, I'd cast my cares on the Lord. But if all I felt was fear, I'd snatch control back from Him. One moment I was surrendering and giving control to Jesus. The next moment I was taking it back.

Here's the thing I learned throughout that process: Faith is not about feelings. It's about deciding to trust in what you can't see or fully comprehend. And when I made the conscious choice to trust God with my future, His gentle nudges began to guide me.

His voice didn't scold me for my doubts; instead, He reminded me I was His beloved daughter and He loved me unconditionally. Whether through the Scriptures, worship songs, or the wisdom of others (like my pastor's wife), God's presence was always there, gently leading me forward.

From the Struggle to the Dance

Despite these insights, there still were moments when impatience got the best of me. We've all been there, haven't we? We wonder why God is taking so long to work on our behalf. And in those moments of frustration, we often try to take matters into our own hands—only to mess things up even more. It's like we toss the ball back into God's court, demanding answers for His seeming inaction.

One morning at the pergola, I was struggling to see how anything good could ever work out. By now, it had been almost three weeks since I had last heard from Andrew, and my anxiety was creeping in again. I was doing my best to surrender my fears and give control to Jesus. During this moment of desperation, I stumbled across some of my old journals. As someone who has always cherished the practice of journaling, I felt a profound gratitude for preserving these precious records of my journey. As I flipped through the pages, my eyes landed on an entry from thirteen years earlier. In it, I had poured out my heart to the Lord and written down the whispers of guidance that I felt deep within me:

"I am the Lord of the dance. Let me lead, and you learn to follow me."

I read these words over and over again, letting them sink in.

"I am the Lord of the dance. Let me lead, and you learn to follow me."

As I meditated on the words from my journal, I realized I had lost track of the music playing softly in the background. It was a familiar tune, one that tugged at my heartstrings. The song was called "Dance with Me" by Paul Wilbur. Curious, I reached for my phone and turned up the volume, listening intently to the lyrics. It speaks of dancing with the lover of my soul and is an intimate invitation for God to romance me as His cherished bride.

The message of the song seemed tailor-made for just this moment. The words I had penned in my journal more than thirteen years earlier sounded much like the ones I was hearing now. Could it be that God was orchestrating the exact timing of this song, speaking to me through these lyrics?

I sank to my knees, pouring out my heart in prayer, a desperate plea for God to mend the shattered pieces within me. "Lord, forgive my attempts to take control. Show me how to trust You truly," I whispered, my voice trembling with sincerity. "Would You join me in this dance as the song suggests? I'm ready to surrender every piece of my heart to You."

I sat in stillness, not sure what came next. In the quiet, a gentle voice echoed within me and lovingly invited, "Put your feet on top of mine and watch what I can do."

With hesitant steps, I rose and moved to the center of the pergola. Raising my arms in the graceful arc of a waltz, I stood poised in surrender and allowed my soul to be led in silent conversation with my Creator. With my eyes closed and my face upturned toward heaven, this dance became an intimate offering, a sacred act of devotion to my audience of one.

As the final notes faded away, I bowed my head in reverence, silently acknowledging the holiness that surrounded me. Any doubts vanished. I knew I was standing on holy ground.

From that day forward, my mornings began with the familiar ritual of surrender, a dance between my soul and my Creator. I would stand there alone and find solace as I imagined God's strong arms embracing me. As an act of faith, I raised my arms in invitation, allowing the music to envelop me in prayerful communion. And as the final strains of the song faded, I'd bow my head and curtsy in a silent gesture of respect and gratitude.

Trust God's Plan

Trusting God's leadership also means trusting His plan. Proverbs 19:21 reminds us that while we may devise our own plans, ultimately "it is the LORD's purpose that prevails." Isaiah 55:9 reinforces this, highlighting the vast difference between God's thoughts and our own. His plans for us far exceed our human understanding, guiding us toward paths we may never have imagined.

So, how do we trust God's plan? Proverbs 16:3 says, "Commit to the LORD whatever you do, and he will establish your plans." According to *Ellicott's Commentary for English Readers*, the phrase "commit thy works unto the Lord" (KJV) literally means to roll them upon Him as a burden too heavy to be carried yourself. Our plans will prosper because "they will be undertaken according to the will of God, and carried out by His aid."[2]

One way we commit our plans to God is by casting our cares on the Lord. Psalm 55:22 tells us, "Cast your burden upon the LORD and He will sustain you; He will never allow the righteous to be shaken" (NASB). Anytime I think of casting something, I go back to a time in my childhood when my parents owned and operated a remote fly-in fishing camp in northern Ontario. One thing I learned to do well was catch fish. I had my very own rod and reel, knew how to bait my hook, and spent many hours practicing my technique of casting my line into the water. I held the fishing pole firmly in one hand and used the thumb on my other hand to release the tension on the reel so the fishing line went flying. With my pole high over my head, I let my line soar through the air until I heard it plop into the water. Again and again, I'd cast out my line and reel it back in to see if I had caught a fish.

> Trusting God's leadership also means trusting His plan.

Casting our cares on the Lord is a lot like releasing our fishing line into the air and having no control over where it lands. God desires that we let go and trust His ability to handle our problems rather than reeling our anxieties and cares back in. Too often, though, we find ourselves getting impatient when we feel God isn't working fast enough on our behalf. That's when we slip back into our control mode and begin to reel our worries back in.

Do you, like me, struggle with releasing burdens you hold dear? Is it challenging for you to entrust certain people in your life to God? Perhaps it's a spouse or a child, and you fear that if you stop worrying about them, the Lord will forget to give them His attention. Or maybe it is a daunting health diagnosis that threatens to overwhelm your faith.

No matter what life throws your way, fear will often try to convince you that God won't show up on the scene, won't see you, and won't see you through. Fear is like a relentless night watchman that keeps you awake with incessant worries and whispers of doubt. It makes you feel like it's up to you to figure everything out just in case God doesn't have a plan. But 2 Timothy 1:7 says, "For God has not given us a spirit of fear, but of power and of love and of a sound mind" (NKJV).

Sweet friend, God wants you to know that fear is nothing but a liar!

The Burdens We Carry

Not long after my divorce, I began to struggle with debilitating fear. Having a sound mind was, at that time, the furthest thing from my truth. I worried about my children and whether they would be okay. I worried about my finances and how I would survive as a single mom. I worried about whether I was doomed to be alone for the rest of my life. And I worried about whether I would emotionally have what it took to keep my job.

At the time of my divorce, I was working as a therapist at a small nonprofit agency. I was on the verge of emotional burnout and knew I had to get away for a break to restore my spirit. I didn't know where to go, so one day I just got in my car and drove toward a nearby town where I knew there was a lake. Because of those summers I had spent in northern Canada, being around water always had a calming effect on my soul.

After driving for what seemed to be the better part of an hour, I spotted a boat dock. I parked my car, reached for my journal, and walked toward the waiting water. The sun's reflection glistened like millions of twinkling lights. I watched as birds flew in formation.

When I got to the dock, I opened my journal to the first empty page. Not sure where to begin, I took my pen and began to trace my hand just like I used to do when I was a kid. When I finished the outline, I moved my hand and stared at this makeshift hand-print. Next, I wrote the words that had been weighing so heavily on my heart.

On the pinkie finger I wrote "weary."

On the ring finger I wrote "fear of the future."

On the middle finger I wrote "lonely."

On the pointer finger I wrote "anxiety."

On the thumb I wrote "hopeless."

Finally, in the center of the hand I scribbled "hurt" and "anger."

I noticed that to trace my hand, I had to lay it flat against the paper with my palm facing down. I sat in silence for a while until a gentle whisper stirred in my heart, nudging me to let go of those burdens: *When your open palm is held out in front of you with your palm facing the ground, there is no way this hand can hold on to anything. Everything falls out of an open palm that is facing down. The emotions you wrote on your outlined hand are the same emotions I want you to let go of.*

I picked up my pen and traced a second hand, but this one I filled with promises from God's Word. Promises of rest, hope, companionship, peace, assurance, and forgiveness.

Where I had written "weary," I now wrote, "Come to Me, all who are weary and burdened, and I will give you rest" (Matt. 11:28 NASB).

Where I had written "fear of the future," I now wrote, "'For I know the plans I have for you,' declares the LORD, 'plans to prosper you and not to harm you, plans to give you hope and a future'" (Jer. 29:11).

Where I had written "lonely," I now wrote, "The LORD is close to the brokenhearted and saves those who are crushed in spirit" (Ps. 34:18) and "Draw near to God and He will draw near to you" (James 4:8 NKJV).

Where I had written "anxiety," I now wrote, "Be anxious for nothing, but in everything by prayer and supplication, with thanksgiving, let your requests be made known to God; and the peace of God, which surpasses all understanding, will guard your hearts and minds through Christ Jesus" (Phil. 4:6–7 NKJV).

Where I had written "hopeless," I now wrote, "For God alone, O my soul, wait in silence, for my hope is from him. He only is my rock and my salvation, my fortress; I shall not be shaken" (Ps. 62:5–6 ESV).

Finally, where I had written "hurt" and "anger," I now wrote, "Get rid of all bitterness, rage and anger, brawling and slander, along with every form of malice. Be kind and compassionate to one another, forgiving each other, just as in Christ God forgave you" (Eph. 4:31–32).

As I completed this exercise, something shifted within me, as if a weight had been lifted off my shoulders. Each promise I wrote down brought a sense of peace and relief. I realized that by turning those burdens over to the Lord and changing my way of thinking from focusing on my problems to focusing on the Lord and what He says, I could find true healing. It was a transformative moment, one that brought clarity and hope to my heart amid the turmoil of emotions.

Trust God's Timing

In addition to trusting God's leadership and plan for our lives, we need to trust God's timing. This is something I have wrestled with for years. My impatience has earned me playful comparisons to Veruca Salt, a character from the classic movie *Willy Wonka & the Chocolate Factory* who is best known for her line, "Daddy, I want it NOW!"[3] But seriously, this is a lesson I learned the hard way: God's timing and my timing are usually not the same. His clock ticks differently than mine.

This lesson reminds me of a time in my early twenties when I decided to plant a garden. I was newly married and living in our first home. I drove to the nearby hardware store and bought packets of tomato seeds. I tilled and prepared the soil, putting seeds into the small holes I dug. I watered the seeds every morning and expectantly watched for any signs of growth. After five days of not seeing anything, I got my trowel and dug them back up to see what was going on beneath the soil.

I hadn't read the seed packet, so I hadn't considered the fact that while a tomato seed can germinate in six to ten days under ideal conditions, the average tomato plant can take sixty to a hundred days to fully grow. Only five days in I was already digging up seeds that had not yet begun to sprout. I repeated this process every few days. Needless to say, I killed the plants. My impatience had gotten the better of me. What I needed to learn was that just because I didn't see signs of growth above the soil didn't mean things weren't happening beneath the surface. That's a lot like our journey with God. Just because we don't see something happening with our eyes doesn't mean God isn't acting on our behalf behind the scenes.

Psalm 37:34 reminds us, "*Wait for the Lord and keep his way*" (ESV). Don't rush God's timing. His plans will unfold in His own perfect rhythm. Psalm 27:14 repeats that phrase for emphasis: "*Wait on the LORD*; be of good courage, and He shall strengthen your heart; *wait, I say, on the LORD!*" (NKJV). How often do we find ourselves getting in front of God's timetable simply because we grow weary of waiting for Him to act? As Psalm 106:13 states, "But they soon forgot what he had done and did not wait for his plan to unfold." Indeed, the most challenging part of trusting God is often in the times of waiting.

Trust God's Heart

Trusting God's heart is not just about believing in His goodness but also about finding deep rest in His care. My best friend once shared this profound truth with me: *If we aren't resting, we're not truly trusting, and if we're not trusting, we're not genuinely resting.* Trust and rest are inseparable, intertwined in a beautiful tandem dance. You can't have one without the other.

This truth became even more evident to me following my assault. During the attack, my ex-husband had aimed his gun at my bedroom wall and unleashed three terrifying shots. Two days later, I found myself standing in awe at the scene. There in the middle of my wall, where I'd hung a rectangular sign with a decorative verse, resounded the words of Exodus 14:14 amid all the evidence of that morning's chaos and fear:

The LORD will fight for you; you need only to be still.

The words echoed in my mind, offering a glimmer of hope in the darkness. As I examined the wall, I noticed the precise placement of the bullet holes—one above the sign and two directly below it. The sign itself remained miraculously untouched, a tangible reminder of God's unwavering protection and provision.

Five days after the assault, I received the following message from a woman I worked with:

Kim,
I sit here in my living room working on notes, and this is a place where I feel safe. All I can think about is you. You are on my mind almost constantly! It breaks my heart to know safety has been taken away from you and so much

more. I can't imagine what you are going through. I have been praying for you and your family, and thank the Lord you are still here and will overcome this. I don't know what words to say to comfort you, and I'm not gonna try, but I just want to say sorry. Sorry this happened to you. I pray that you will find comfort in our Lord and that you will feel His presence and His arms wrapped around you. I pray for healing and strength. You are one of the strongest women I know. Please know we are all thinking of you during this extremely difficult time! I couldn't sleep thinking about you and so I had to reach out. I will leave you with this because it keeps coming to me. Exodus 14:14: "The Lord will fight for you; you need only to be still." These words may seem so simple and plain, but they are so powerful!

Love you!

K[4]

Her words sent shivers up and down my spine. This friend had never been inside my home, and we hadn't spent much one-on-one time together. She had no idea about that Scripture sign hanging on my wall. She couldn't have known how bullets had pierced the space around it just days earlier. But it was unmistakable to me: God was once again speaking directly to my heart.

In my life, I've experienced firsthand how God fights for His children. I've also witnessed it in the lives of others, and I've come to realize that He doesn't always fight for us in the ways we expect or envision. In my case, it looked like Him keeping me alive in a difficult situation. As a child, I had prayed for God to cover me with a "cake pan" of protection, and in my moment of gravest danger He did just that and spared my life. He intervened by giving me a strong inclination to lock my bedroom door. It seemed like a small action at the time, but it turned out to be lifesaving. If the sound of my door crashing down hadn't woken me, my ex-husband, in his intoxicated state, might have stood over my sleeping body and killed me. God's defending us can come in unexpected ways, but His faithfulness never wavers.

The Contemporary English Version translates Exodus 14:14 as, "The LORD will fight for you, and you won't have to do a thing." God's role is to fight on our behalf, and our part is to trust Him and allow Him to work, even when it's difficult to understand His methods.

Trusting God is an active choice—a declaration of faith in His unwavering love and power. We learn to trust by declaring His Word. Even when doubt creeps in, we can reinforce our trust by speaking it out loud. So, in the middle of uncertainty, remind yourself again and again. Say it until your heart believes it: Lord, I choose to trust You!

PAUSE AND REFLECT

- Surrendering control becomes easier when we trust the one in charge, especially if it's someone we already know. Take a few moments to assess your current relationship with the Lord. Are you investing time in reading His Word, praying, and worshiping Him? Identify any areas that need improvement and develop a plan to prioritize them.

- Embark on a journey of self-discovery and spiritual connection by starting a journal. Pour out your thoughts, prayers, and reflections onto the pages, allowing yourself to express the emotions you're feeling inside. Dedicate a few minutes each day to writing, opening yourself to the insights and guidance that may unfold as you share your heart with God. (See "The Power of Journaling" in the Tools for Growth and Healing.)

- Where do you find it hard to let go of control in your life? Is it your family, children, spouse, parents, finances, job, health, future, or dreams? What burdens are you still carrying that you need to give to God? Take a moment to share your struggles with Him.

- Grab a piece of paper and place your hand on it, tracing its outline with your palm facing down. On each finger, write down a fear you have about various situations. For example, "Worrying about my child's choices." Then, have a conversation with God and hand over these fears to Him. Next, take another piece of paper and trace your hand once more. This time, instead of writing down fears, search your Bible for promises that address each fear. Write these promises on each finger and keep this paper where you can easily see it. For the next week, whenever worry starts to creep in, remind yourself of the promises you've written down.

—————— PRAYER OF OUR HEART ——————

Lord, more than anything, I desire to learn to trust You. If I'm honest, there are times when I'm afraid to let go of those things I worry about. Please show me how to trust You. I repent of the times I've tried to fight You for control. Right now, at this moment, I lift my open hands to You as a sign of my surrender. You promise You'll fight these battles for me. Please teach me how to be still and rest in Your presence. Help me to understand that You're not asking for my help; You're asking for my heart. I say out loud that I am choosing to trust You. And when my heart wavers, I will choose to say it again and again until it becomes real in my life. I surrender my life to You, Jesus! In Your mighty name I pray. Amen.

8

A TIME TO FORGIVE

Tell Your Heart to Beat Again

Forgiveness is an act of the will, and the will can function regardless of the temperature of the heart.

CORRIE TEN BOOM

Then Peter came to Jesus and asked, "Lord, how many times shall I forgive my brother or sister who sins against me? Up to seven times?" Jesus answered, "I tell you, not seven times, but seventy-seven times."

MATTHEW 18:21–22

I don't know anyone who just *loves* to forgive. That's because if you find yourself needing to forgive, it means you're the one who's been wounded. If we don't handle these hurts in a healthy way, they can turn into anger. Left unresolved, this anger festers into resentment and unforgiveness, leaving us to go through life as the walking wounded.

That's exactly where I found myself in the year leading up to my divorce. A few months earlier, I had discovered my husband of twenty-two years had been having an affair. On the one hand, I desperately wanted to see if our marriage could be salvaged for the sake of our children, and I tried to convince myself that forgiveness was the only answer. On the other hand, anger simmered beneath the surface, and I'd lash out and say things to sting him just as he'd stung me with his betrayal. It seemed like a never-ending cycle of pain and bitterness.

One Sunday morning during that time, we went to church together as a family. Within that worshipful atmosphere, I stood beside my husband in the pew and struggled to find peace from the turmoil I felt on the inside. As the congregation raised their hands in worship, I felt anything but peace. Even the music couldn't drown my racing thoughts. When the music ended, everything got quiet while the congregation prepared for the customary prayer before the pastor began his sermon. Suddenly, an inner voice broke through the chaos of my thoughts with a clear message:

You need to forgive her.

I knew it was the Lord speaking.

151

As the words reverberated in my mind, a wave of emotions crashed over me. My stomach knotted and anger surged through my veins. I knew exactly who "her" referred to—the woman my husband had betrayed me with. The mere thought of forgiving her felt like an impossible demand. How could God expect me to forgive the person who had torn my family apart? Didn't He see the devastation *she* had caused *me*? I was the innocent one! I gripped the pew so tightly that my knuckles turned white.

Over the previous months, bitterness had slowly woven its threads into my heart. Looking back on the situation later, I was reminded of a lesson I had often taught my young children as we tended to our backyard each spring. We'd meticulously clear away weeds and leaves the wind had left behind. We'd prune the bushes and trim the trees, readying them for the upcoming season. There were always a number of pesky vines sneaking over the privacy fence that separated our neighbor's yard from ours. The creeping vines would entangle themselves with the healthy branches of our beloved crepe myrtle trees.

"Kids," I'd say, pointing to the invading vines, "this is how sin works. If you don't guard your hearts and minds, sin will weave its way in, choking out the good things God has planned for you."

And here I stood, years later, facing my own tangled mess. Vines of bitterness and resentment had wrapped themselves around my heart, closing it off and hardening it.

Once more the unmistakable voice echoed in my soul: *You need to forgive her.*

That's when the dialogue between me and the Lord began.

"But I don't want to forgive her!" I inwardly argued.

"Why can you forgive your husband but not her?" came His gentle reply.

"Because I love my husband, but I hate her! I don't love her, Lord!"

And that's when He replied, "But I do."

Over the next days, weeks, and months, my heart wrestled with God repeatedly. I told Him that He didn't understand what He was asking of me. I questioned if He'd seen how I'd been treated. After all, *I* hadn't done anything wrong. *I* was the one in the right. How could God possibly expect *me* to forgive *her*?

Misconceptions About Forgiveness

Perhaps we battle with this idea of forgiveness because we don't understand what forgiveness truly means. We mistake forgiving for dismissing or forgetting the wrongs committed against us. We think of forgiveness as "giving in" or "giving up" while the other person "gets away." We put it in terms of winning versus losing, and we view the one who forgives as powerless and weak. We tell ourselves we'll forgive when we feel like it, only to find ourselves continually waiting for a feeling that never comes.

We may also resist the idea of forgiveness because we feel justified in our anger since we are the ones who were hurt. What begins as a feeling of justification morphs into pride. We say things like, "I didn't deserve this" and "I'm better than the person who wronged me." We take pleasure in telling others how we were wronged and thrive on the sympathy of anyone who voices agreement. We ask others to take our side and wear our hurt as a badge of honor.

And then there's the misconception that forgiveness means we have to welcome the person who hurt us back into our lives, opening ourselves to potential harm again. Fearful of future pain, we can withhold forgiveness because of the mistaken belief that it necessitates a restoration of trust.

None of the above ideas about forgiveness are accurate, and when we believe these things, we are playing right into Satan's hands. Satan wants nothing more than to harden our hearts with bitterness and unforgiveness. Much like the hardening of our physical arteries obstructs blood flow to the heart, unforgiveness obstructs the flow of love and grace in our soul, leading to a spiritual heart attack. The devil's lies poison our hearts with fear, anger, and resentment. Left unchecked, these blockages build, erecting walls that separate us from God and others. We may not consciously choose to distance ourselves from God, but through our daily decisions and thoughts, we find ourselves drifting further from Him. We cease to pray and engage with His Word. We withdraw from worship and intimacy with Him. We may continue to go through the motions, but we withhold our hearts. Instead we internalize and succumb to the devil's deceitful narrative that God has failed us.

The Truth About Forgiveness

God never asks us to do something He hasn't done Himself. He knows we are capable of forgiveness because He designed us with the capacity to forgive. God not only gave us the ability to forgive but also set Himself as the ultimate example when He chose to extend forgiveness to us. John 3:16, perhaps the most familiar verse in the Bible, illustrates this truth: "For God so loved the world, that he gave his only begotten Son, that whosoever believeth in him should not perish, but have everlasting life" (KJV).

> God never asks us to do something He hasn't done Himself.

God's forgiveness came at a great cost. He sacrificed His only Son to redeem us. If God, who is blameless, will forgive us for the offenses we commit, then who are we to withhold forgiveness from others? Though you may feel justified in holding on to offenses, remember that Jesus, innocent and faultless, bore the weight of our transgressions. He endured unfair accusations and ultimately paid with His life.

Here's the truth about forgiveness:

Forgiveness isn't a punishment for us. It's a liberating gift that sets us free.

Forgiveness isn't a feeling we wait for. It's a deliberate choice
we get to make.

Forgiveness isn't the same as trust. It doesn't mean unhealthy
relationships must be restored. It means we get to establish
healthy boundaries to keep ourselves safe.

Forgiveness isn't "one and done." It's a process we get to
walk through.

Forgiveness isn't easy. God's grace comes alongside to help
us.

Forgiveness doesn't mean forgetting. It means choosing not
to dwell on past pain.

Forgiveness isn't giving in or giving up while the other person
gets away. It's allowing God to be the one who rights every
wrong.

Forgiveness is much like a scar. A scar indicates that something happened, that you were hurt. The pain you felt
from the initial injury is gone. The wound is no longer
gaping, open, or hurting. The scar bears witness to your
pain and serves as evidence that your hurt is now healed.

Why Forgive?

Why does God instruct us to forgive others? It's simple: because
He loves us and wants nothing more than to extend His forgiveness
to us. In Mark 11:25, Jesus says, "Whenever you stand praying, if
you have anything against anyone, forgive him [drop the issue, let
it go], so that your Father who is in heaven will also forgive you
your transgressions and wrongdoings [against Him and others]"
(AMP).

When we refuse to forgive others, we limit our relationship with
God. Unforgiveness is a barrier, a sin that erects walls between
us and God. In essence, by refusing to forgive, we're choosing to
block ourselves off from the very source of forgiveness and healing.

Moreover, unforgiveness traps us in the past, replaying old hurts and grievances in our minds. It drains our energy and steals our joy as we constantly dwell on what was done to us. Our brains fixate on the details, hoping to protect us from future harm, but instead we become stuck in bitterness and resentment.

So, when we forgive, we not only open ourselves to receive God's forgiveness but also free ourselves from the burdens of the past. We tear down the walls we erected and reclaim our joy and peace.

What About When They Don't Say "I'm Sorry"?

A person who refuses to forgive hurts only themselves. As Anne Lamott so eloquently put it, "Not forgiving is like drinking rat poison and then waiting for the rat to die."[1] By choosing to hold on to our pain, we stay stuck in the past while the one who wronged us moves on. By choosing to forgive, we unshackle ourselves from the past and embrace freedom to move forward.

I'm reminded of a time when my daughter was a toddler and still in diapers. Whenever I finished changing her poopy diaper, she'd grab the dirty diaper, hold it to her chest, and make a run for it. She'd look at us and smile, then squeal the word, "Mine!" No matter how stinky the diaper was, it was hers, and she was not about to part with it.

Many of us cling to our feelings of offense the way my daughter clung to those dirty diapers. Despite how much these feelings stink, no matter how deeply they harm us, we hold on to them and declare, "Mine!" Our pride and stubbornness prevent us from letting go of unforgiveness. We convince ourselves that we'll only forgive if the person who hurt us comes forward with a sincere apology. Even then, we often make them grovel until we're satisfied their remorse is genuine.

You may be familiar with the story in Genesis about twin brothers Esau and Jacob. Many Bible teachers focus on their father, Isaac, but I'm particularly interested in what the brothers' relationship can teach us about forgiveness. As you may recall, Esau and Jacob's rivalry began at birth (see Gen. 25:19–26). In the ancient world, it was customary for a father to give his patriarchal blessing to his firstborn son. This blessing entailed leadership, authority, and a double portion of the inheritance. As the older twin, Esau was the rightful heir to these privileges.

One day, Jacob decided to seize an opportunity to trick Esau into giving up his birthright for a bowl of stew (Gen. 25:27–34). In a moment of weakness, Esau agreed. Then, when it came time for Isaac to proclaim the patriarchal blessing, Jacob disguised himself as Esau and tricked their father into giving him the blessing. Once Esau learned what happened, he was angry and began plotting his revenge, prompting Jacob to flee in fear for his life (Gen. 27).

> Forgiveness doesn't depend on what another person says or does. It's an attitude of **your** heart and a choice **you** make to let go of an offense.

After twenty years passed, the Lord told Jacob to return to his homeland. Fearing Esau's wrath and retribution, Jacob sent ahead gifts for his brother as a peace offering (Gen. 32:1–23). Esau's response, however, took Jacob by surprise.

In Genesis 33 we're told that when Esau saw his younger brother coming toward him, he "ran to meet him and embraced him, threw his arms around his neck, and kissed him. And they both wept" (v. 4 NLT). Instead of spewing anger and resentment at Jacob, Esau embraced him with love and forgiveness. Though he had every right to be mad at his brother, somewhere along the way God had softened Esau's heart, causing him to forgive his brother *even though Jacob had never asked.*

I often think of this story when I'm asked if it's possible to forgive someone who hasn't said they're sorry. My answer is always a wholehearted "Yes!" Forgiveness doesn't depend on what another person says or does. It's an attitude of *your* heart and a choice *you* make to let go of an offense.

The account of Jacob and Esau is a beautiful testimony of how God can soften even the hardest of hearts and redeem what the enemy has meant for evil in our lives. God can restore relationships that need to be restored, and redemption truly is possible.

Whom Should I Forgive?

God has called us to forgive everyone.

I don't know if it's just me, but I find that some people are way easier to forgive than others. One determining factor is the depth of our relationship with the person who hurt us. In my case, I had to forgive people I hated just as much as I had to forgive people I loved.

The ultimate example of forgiveness is found in Jesus's words on the cross when He pleaded, "Father, forgive them, for they do not know what they are doing" (Luke 23:34). Notice that Jesus didn't pray, "Father, give these people what they deserve." Instead, Jesus surrendered His right to vengeance and freely offered forgiveness.

Like Jesus, we are called to entrust our grievances to God, believing He will make all things right. For me, in the months and years following my ex-husband's betrayal, this meant I had to trust not only that God *could* heal my heart but that He *would* heal my heart. Trusting and committing my grievances to God following the assault looked much the same. In both cases, I knew the choice was mine: Would I submit my will and emotions to Him?

I knew my journey to forgiveness wouldn't be easy, but it was necessary. I needed to forgive other people I felt had contributed to my troubles. I needed to forgive the woman my husband had betrayed me with, as well as to forgive my ex-husband. And I also needed to forgive myself and God if I was going to obtain healing and restoration in my life.

Forgiving "Them"

Throughout my twenty-three years of marriage, both before and after my husband's betrayal, I was inundated with what was considered "godly" advice from members of my church community. I was constantly hearing sermons about holding on and trusting God to heal marriages, yet few of these addressed the importance of setting healthy boundaries or recognizing when self-preservation should take precedence.

In the year leading up to my divorce, as I faced the reality of my husband's infidelity, I grappled with the decision of whether to stay or leave. With the best of intentions, people around me offered their unsolicited advice, believing they were helping me navigate the right path. Unfortunately, their counsel only made things worse. Despite their genuine concern, they lacked a full understanding of my circumstances, yet I allowed their words to sway me. As a result, after my assault, I held on to bitterness toward those who had urged me to remain so long in a situation that ultimately harmed me.

Through this experience, I learned that seeing through a lens of understanding and compassion can help release anger and resentment. Recognizing that people make mistakes and often act from their own limited perspectives can pave the way for healing and forgiveness. This realization helped me to forgive those who had misled me, and it is a path that others can follow too. By embracing empathy and acknowledging our shared humanity, we can let go of offenses and find peace.

Forgiving "Her"

Discovering that my husband had been having an affair for the year leading up to our divorce was undoubtedly one of the toughest hurdles I had to face. While I knew Scripture says to pray for those who hurt us (Matt. 5:44), the last thing I wanted to do was pray for the woman involved. Though I knew my husband was as much to blame for the affair, all I could think of was how I wanted her to hurt as much as she had hurt me.

I'm not proud when I say that in my darkest moments I secretly wished for her misfortune or downfall. In my whole life, I had never known such hate for another person. The pages of my journal were filled with anger and rage toward this woman. If I had to pray for her, I only wanted to pray that God would cause her unhappiness, pain, and hurt. My ugly attitude toward this woman just kept getting worse.

One Sunday morning shortly after my divorce, I snuck into the back row of the church, hoping to go unnoticed. The pastor announced the church sanctuary was going to be repainted soon. Before the walls were covered with fresh paint, he invited everyone in the church to take a black Sharpie and write the names of people who needed the Lord on the wall. People could pray over these names each time they entered the building, and even after the walls were repainted, those names would remain an unseen testament to the power of prayer.

I soon found myself wrestling with an inner voice that I had come to recognize as the prompting of the Lord.

"I want you to write her name on the wall," the voice urged.

"No," I inwardly replied.

There was no way I was going to write her name on the wall. I did not want to pray for her myself, and I didn't want anyone else to pray for her either. I told myself I wanted her to die a sinner.

"Go write her name on the wall," I heard again.

Feeling a strong sense of conviction, this time I didn't argue. With shaky hands and a heavy heart, I chose to obey. I took the marker and etched her name on the sanctuary wall. That moment was less about forgiveness and more about admitting I needed to let go of my anger and give it to the Lord.

It's important to understand that this act didn't instantly make all my anger go away. It was just the beginning of a journey toward forgiveness that the Lord led me through. Eventually, I was able to truly forgive this woman, especially after my assault.

If those church walls could talk, they would tell you the story of two women Jesus loves: me *and* her. His love for us is equal. We are both His daughters and we both need His love and forgiveness.

Forgiving "Him"

Throughout our twenty-three years of marriage, forgiving my husband was a regular part of my life. Despite his recurring lies and betrayals, I held on to hope, fueled by an enduring love and a belief in his potential to change. However, the painful reality of his continued behavior eventually gave me the courage to step away from our toxic relationship.

On the tragic morning of my assault, my ex-husband faced the consequences of his actions as he looked down into my bloodied face. As his intoxication began to wear off, the gravity of what he had just done started to sink in. Meeting my gaze, he spoke with a weighty sense of resignation, acknowledging the irreparable damage he had caused.

"Tell me. I've gone too far this time. We could never go back. You could never forgive me," he said.

With little to no hesitation, a clear mind, and all sincerity, I solemnly responded, "You're right. You've gone too far this time. We can never go back. But I want you to know that I do and will forgive you."

These words, spoken during pain and suffering, would be some of the final words I would ever speak to him.

On the day my ex-husband assaulted me and tried to kill Andrew, the police arrested him and took him to jail. As darkness fell that night, I found myself praying for my ex-husband. I prayed that he wouldn't feel alone or frightened in his jail cell. I prayed that he would somehow sense the presence of God with him. And in that moment, I realized that I truly meant every word I was praying.

I can't say I understand why my ex-husband did what he did to Andrew and me, and nothing would ever excuse his actions. I have, however, come to understand the saying that "hurt people hurt people." By forgiving my ex-husband, I did not absolve him of his wrongdoing. Rather, the choice to forgive him was rooted in my own healing journey. My decision enabled me to release the burden of bitterness and resentment that threatened to consume me.

While forgiveness does not erase the memories of my pain, it provides me the freedom to move forward with grace and resilience. In that moment, I forgave my ex-husband, but I knew I would have to remind myself to forgive him each time the pain resurfaced. When memories of the hurt emerge, I reaffirm my decision to forgive. This continual act of forgiveness allows me to reclaim my peace and strength and ensures that my past does not dictate my future.

Since that time, my prayer has not changed. I continue to pray that my ex-husband finds healing in his life as he serves out his prison sentence and allows God—who loves him every bit as much as He loves me—to become very real to him in the days, months, and years ahead.

Forgiving Ourselves

Sometimes, it's easier to forgive ourselves than it is to forgive others. I've heard it said that we judge others by their actions but ourselves by our intentions. We excuse and minimize our behaviors by saying, "I didn't mean to." Yet when others say that to us, we often respond with, "I don't care what you meant to do; you hurt me!" Other times, however, we are quick to forgive others but refuse to give ourselves the same grace. We hold things we've said or done against ourselves and beat ourselves up for our mistakes.

Forgiving myself was the hardest thing to do. After my divorce, I felt ashamed for every little mistake I convinced myself I had made in my marriage. I kept telling myself I should've been smarter and not trusted again so soon, and that I should've done things differently rather than blindly forgiving and looking the other way. Instead of seeing my mistakes as mistakes, I told myself I had failed and hurt everyone in my path. I let myself believe the devil's lies that told me not only had I failed but I was a complete failure.

To forgive myself, I had to let go of the lies I had come to believe about my worth and my role in my marriage. I had judged myself for not setting healthier boundaries that could have protected me and my children from harm. I had to extend forgiveness to myself for the decisions I had made, particularly for staying in an unhealthy marriage as long as I did.

I had to forgive myself for falling short of the impossible standard of being the "perfect wife." Shame made me believe that if I had been a better wife, my husband wouldn't have cheated. I also felt guilty for what I saw as failing my kids. Despite my efforts to keep my family whole, the divorce meant they were now from a broken home. Finally, I had to forgive myself for what I perceived as letting God down by not keeping my vow of "till death do us part."

I'd allowed myself to believe all these things that simply weren't true. There's no such thing as the perfect wife; it's an unrealistic standard. I didn't fail my children; I made decisions with their well-being as my priority. And I didn't disappoint God; His love and grace enveloped me. It wasn't His plan for me to remain in a toxic and unfaithful relationship.

> Forgiving ourselves means relinquishing the self-condemnation and shame we bear for past mistakes.

In John 8, Jesus offered a profound example of forgiveness when He encountered a woman accused of adultery: "Then Jesus stood up again and said to the woman, 'Where are your accusers? Didn't even one of them condemn you?' 'No, Lord,' she said" (vv. 10–11 NLT). Forgiving ourselves means relinquishing the self-condemnation and shame we bear for past mistakes. It means recognizing that Jesus bore the weight of our shame on the cross and has set us free from its burden. Jesus died to cover all our shame—every mistake we have made in the past and every mistake we have yet to make in the future.

Forgiving God

When I talk about our need to forgive God, let me clarify: God doesn't need our forgiveness. But that doesn't mean we don't still need to forgive Him. We forgive for our sake, not His. Most of us have been guilty of holding God to our own human standards. We've expected Him to answer our prayers the way we want, and when that doesn't happen, we are disappointed and blame God for everything bad that happens.

One of the most common reasons people say they don't believe in God anymore is because they feel He has let them down. We feel abandoned when God doesn't intervene the way we think He is supposed to: He didn't save a loved one's life. He didn't mend our broken family. He didn't rescue us from financial ruin. He didn't step in and get us the job we wanted. He didn't miraculously heal our body. And the list goes on and on.

In our frustration, we often blame God for things He isn't guilty of. We place ourselves in the seat of both judge and jury, holding Him accountable for our pain and suffering. This plays right into Satan's hands as he revels in our anger toward God. Satan's ultimate goal is to make us doubt God's love so we will walk away from our relationship with Him.

If this is the case with you right now, I encourage you to pause for a moment and pray. Be honest with God about your feelings of disappointment. Tell Him you've been angry with Him and feel like He's let you down. Tell Him you don't understand why He didn't answer your prayer how and when you wanted Him to. Humbly ask Him to forgive you for walking away or for becoming distant in your relationship with Him. Then make a conscious choice to release your anger and forgive God for the things you've held against Him. This act of forgiveness can pave the way to healing and restoration in your relationship with Him.

The Journey Toward a Forgiving Heart

Now that we've covered the meaning of forgiveness, why it's important, and when and who we need to forgive, let's dive into the main question: How do we actually forgive? Here are some steps to guide us on the path to healing and forgiveness:

Be honest with God. Bring your pain to God and tell Him exactly how you feel. Prayer is a place for honesty, not performance or perfection. It's okay to say, "God, I'm so mad at that person and I don't want to forgive. I'm asking You to help me become willing."

Be honest with yourself. Acknowledge your hurt and loss. Grieve it. Just don't allow yourself to get stuck in bitterness. One of the reasons people struggle with forgiveness is they don't feel validated or heard. The good news is that we can validate ourselves. Tell yourself, "I was hurt and it wasn't okay." Name what happened to you. Once you have validated it, choose to release it and let it go.

Quit picking the scab off. For a wound to heal, you have to leave it alone. Each time we ruminate on the wrongs done to us, we pick the scab off a wound that is trying to heal. Apply the ointment of God's Word to your wounds. Each time you're reminded of the pain others inflicted on you, remind yourself that you have chosen to forgive and ask God for His help.

Begin to pray for those who have hurt you. Even when you don't feel like it, pray that God will bring the ones who have hurt you to the foot of the cross where they can find healing. Ask God to help you see them through His eyes of compassion and grace. See those who have harmed you as people just like you who make mistakes.

Recognize that no one deserves forgiveness—not even you. Forgiveness is a gift that we give and receive. Choose to extend it freely.

Refuse to dwell on the offense that caused your injury. When something triggers you and brings the offense back to mind, refuse to ruminate on it. If you dwell on it, the injury is no longer in the past but once again becomes part of the present.

Make a daily choice to forgive. Understand that forgiveness is not a onetime occurrence but an ongoing process. Eventually it will become more natural and you won't need to think about it every day. Sometimes you'll have to forgive again and again for the same hurt. That doesn't mean you allow yourself to continue being hurt by the same people or situations due to a lack of healthy boundaries. Forgiveness means letting go of an offense and letting it stay in the past.

Determine to have empathy for those who have hurt you. Remember that hurt people hurt people. The offense was not a reflection of you. It was a reflection of the one who hurt you. Keeping this in mind makes it easier for you to release the one who wronged you.

Decide to surrender your need to be right. When we believe we are the ones who are justified in our actions, we fight for our right to be right. Forgiveness is not about being fair. It is about freeing yourself from the burden of offense. Decide today to let go of offense. It no longer matters who was in the right.

To forgive yourself, be accountable for your actions and admit your mistakes. Realize that you are human and all humans make mistakes. The important thing is learning from your mistakes. If needed, seek reconciliation with others. When you have done this, receive forgiveness from God.

Forgiveness is a challenging journey, my dear friend. If you find yourself grappling with the need to forgive someone, I encourage you to invite God into the process. It may not be an easy path, but seek His guidance. Ask Him for the wisdom and courage to forgive. And if you've been holding things against yourself, remember that God is a God of redemption who can transform our mistakes into opportunities for growth.

Invite the Lord to perform "open-heart surgery" on you. Where there is hate, bitterness, and resentment in your heart, ask Him to clear the blockages that have held you captive.

Tell Your Heart to Beat Again!

In 2014, Randy Phillips of the renowned group Phillips, Craig, and Dean penned a touching song called "Tell Your Heart to Beat Again."[2] It was inspired by an incredible story involving a pastor and a heart surgeon who was part of his church. The pastor had the rare opportunity to observe the surgeon operate on a member of their congregation.

During the surgery, the surgeon opened the chest cavity, removed the patient's damaged heart, and began to meticulously repair it. When he finished his work and put the heart back in place, it wouldn't start beating again no matter how much he massaged it. Out of options, the surgeon went to the head of the operating table, knelt beside his unconscious patient, and whispered, "This is your surgeon. Your surgery was successful. Your heart has been repaired. Now, tell your heart to beat again."

To the amazement of everyone in the room, the patient's heart began to beat again.

In many ways, we're all like the patient on that operating table. Our hearts have been wounded, and it feels like they are too broken to mend. But the good news is that God is the master heart surgeon. He made our hearts and He knows exactly how to fix them.

If we let Him, He'll break through all the hurt and unforgiveness and make our hearts whole again.

You see, Jesus died on the cross so our hearts could be fully alive again. He wants us to find joy again. He wants us to smile again. He wants us to hope again. And He wants us to laugh again. Just like the surgeon in that operating room, God wants us to agree with Him and tell our heart it's time to come alive again.

Take a moment now and envision Jesus's tender gaze upon you. Hear His loving voice say these words: "My precious child . . . tell your heart to beat again!"

———————— PAUSE AND REFLECT ————————

- Take a moment to quiet your heart and reflect deeply on your experiences. Are there individuals who come to mind that you need to forgive? Perhaps they offered well-intentioned but misguided advice, or maybe their actions were thoughtless and hurtful. Consider the situations where you felt wronged even though you did nothing to deserve it. Take out a piece of paper and write down these names, allowing yourself to acknowledge the hurt they caused.

- Now turn your focus inward. Reflect on your own heart. Have you been holding on to self-blame or refusing to accept the forgiveness that God offers? Add your name to this list and recognize the importance of extending forgiveness to yourself, just as God forgives you.

- Have you found yourself wrestling with anger toward God for perceived wrongs? Maybe you feel let down or abandoned by Him, or perhaps you're questioning why certain things have happened in your life. Acknowledge these feelings and add God's name to your list. Understand that it's okay to express your frustrations and doubts to God.

- When you're ready, lay your hand over the piece of paper where you've written down these names. Take a moment to connect with God, speaking each name to Him one by one. Commit to forgiveness as an act of obedience, trusting in His guidance and grace to help you navigate this process.

- As you move forward, be gentle with yourself. If feelings of anger or unforgiveness resurface, remind yourself of your decision to forgive. Understand that forgiveness is a journey and it's normal to experience moments of struggle along the way. Trust that God understands your heart and knows what justice truly entails. Release the burden of holding on to resentment and allow His peace to fill your spirit.

- For additional resources on forgiveness, see "The Power of Forgiveness" in the Tools for Growth and Healing.

--- PRAYER OF OUR HEART ---

Father God, I ask that You let Your healing forgiveness flow through my veins. Help me to receive Your forgiveness and be willing to forgive myself and others. I choose to be free from condemnation, from strife, and from anger.

I rebuke Satan and won't allow him to hold me hostage anymore! He's a liar and manipulator. I rebuke the shame and lies he has screamed in my ear that I have allowed to hold me down for way too long. Yes, I have made mistakes, but those mistakes are covered under the blood of Jesus. I refuse to be held captive in the prison of my past. Jesus has unlocked my prison doors and set me free. And whom the Son sets free is free indeed. I am free.

I forgive myself for every mistake I've held against myself. I forgive the ones who have hurt me. I declare I will be a person who refuses to hang on to offenses. God, You don't hold unforgiveness for me, so neither will I. I refuse to let my heart grow cold. I refuse to become bitter. Lord, I ask that You give me Your eyes and heart for others. In Jesus's name I pray. Amen.

9

A TIME TO DANCE

Holding On to Your First Love

To heal is to let the Holy Spirit call me to dance, to believe again, even amid my pain, that God will orchestrate and guide my life.

HENRI NOUWEN

You have turned my mourning into joyful dancing.
    You have taken away my clothes of mourning and
        clothed me with joy,
that I might sing praises to you and not be silent.
    O LORD my God, I will give you thanks forever!

PSALM 30:11–12 NLT

The four weeks following the assault felt like an eternity. Andrew's absence and physical healing weighed heavily on my heart as I navigated each day. As I prepared to resume my job, I braced myself for the possibility that Andrew might never reach out to me again. I didn't know where he was, and though I had his phone number, his assistant had told me he didn't want contact, so I respected his space. Despite the ache inside me, I knew I had to keep moving forward. Life had to carry on.

Every morning, I awoke with a resolve to rely on my faith in God. I kept reminding myself of my choice to trust in God's plan even when it felt uncertain. In the midst of the pain and doubt, I decided to hold on to the belief that God had a purpose for me even if I couldn't see or feel it yet.

A few days after my return to work, I received an unexpected phone call from one of my aunts in Canada. Bursting with excitement, she shared a dream that to her felt more like a vision. In this dream, she saw two broken vessels, colorless and shattered. She described how she witnessed Jesus's hand reaching down, gathering the fragments, and crafting them into a single bronze vessel. My aunt fervently believed that these broken vessels symbolized Andrew and me. She was convinced that God would reunite us and transform our shattered lives into something beautiful.

More than anything, I wanted to believe my aunt's hopeful words, but I was hesitant to interpret them as anything more than wishful thinking. Grateful for her encouragement, I tucked her words into my heart and knew that only time would tell.

A few days later, while idly browsing the internet, I stumbled upon a picture of the most stunning turquoise bowl I'd ever seen. It had shiny gold veins snaking through it that caught the light in a mesmerizing way.

Intrigued, I searched to find where it was made and stumbled upon the Japanese art of kintsugi. This method of using gold to repair broken ceramics, known as "golden joinery,"[1] fascinated me. Every piece of kintsugi tells a story. Artisans transform fractures into glistening seams of gold, so each piece is unique. Legend has it that kintsugi dates to fifteenth-century Japan and a shogun's broken tea bowl. The bowl was sent away to be mended, but the shogun was not pleased when it came back stitched together with metal staples. His artisans decided to try a more elegant approach and filled the cracks with radiant gold lacquer, turning the broken bowl into a thing of beauty. The very patches that mend the bowl transform it into something unique and more beautiful than the original.

It's a remarkable metaphor for life—showing that our scars and imperfections can be transformed into something truly magnificent.

From Broken to Beautiful

Many of us have experienced the feeling of being broken beyond repair like shattered pieces of pottery. We've endured the devastating blows of traumatic experiences, grappled with guilt and shame, and felt the weight of loss and grief crack us open. In our brokenness, we've often felt unworthy and irreparably damaged. But Jesus, the Master Craftsman, steps in amid our shattered state. The blood He shed on the cross serves as the liquid gold that fills every crevice, every flaw, and every mistake of our broken imperfection. Jesus not only chooses us but redeems us, restores us, and breathes new life into our fractured souls. Like a meticulous kintsugi artist, He takes our scars and imperfections, once hidden in shame, and transforms us into a masterpiece of unparalleled beauty.

As I sat there at my home desk, captivated by images of kintsugi bowls, my aunt's vision echoed in my mind. Could there be a glimmer of truth to her words? Was it possible that the broken vessels she envisioned represented Andrew and me? Did I dare to let my heart believe this? A flicker of hope burned within me.

> **Jesus not only chooses us but redeems us, restores us, and breathes new life into our fractured souls.**

One evening, just a few days after discovering kintsugi, I found myself seated under the pergola while reflecting on my aunt's dream. A glance at my phone revealed a waiting message from Andrew. My heart raced as I read his opening words: "I'm alive!!"

As I read his words, I felt a mix of relief and apprehension. Knowing he had been shot, I was already on edge, but his account of being shot ten times left me utterly stunned. He ended his short message with a simple, "Take care."

Take care? What did those words imply? Did they signal a goodbye, suggesting he never wanted to see me again? Fueled by adrenaline, I quickly replied. I needed to explain what had happened that day. I needed him to understand that I had prayed for him and done everything I could to keep him safe that day. I had to remind him of the promise he had made.

> Andrew, the night before this happened, I asked if you would fight for me. I had no idea what was about to take place. You wrapped your arms around me, held me, and promised to always fight for me because you said I was worth it. Andrew, I'm asking you to fight for me. I'm asking you to let me fight for you. Please fight for us. Please find your way back to me.

I attached a picture we had taken of ourselves just a few short days before the attack. No sooner had I sent my message than I got his nine-word reply:

> That brings a smile to my face. Thank you.

Fearing this might be my last chance to talk to him, I knew I had to seize the moment and speak directly from my heart.

> Just like I'm worth fighting for, Andrew Haar, you are worth fighting for! And I will be right here waiting for you!

Two days passed without a response, and I found myself incessantly checking my phone, hoping for any sign from Andrew. Finally, on the third day, a message from him broke the silence.

> Good evening. I'm limited in what I can do. I'm in a lot of pain. I go back to surgery early tomorrow morning. Three of my wounds continue to drain and are infected. It sounds like many months of recovery and multiple surgeries ahead. My son is getting me to and from appointments. I have house calls set up, too. Take care.

Take care?! I couldn't believe it. Did he forget how much we had said we meant to each other? His earlier words "I want to marry you" echoed in my mind. My apprehension only grew stronger, and I couldn't shake the guilt weighing on me. I felt responsible for what had happened to him, for his suffering. Knowing he faced multiple surgeries and a long road to recovery added to my worry about his well-being, not just about our relationship.

I responded to his message and offered prayers for his upcoming surgery. His reassurance of reaching out again offered a sliver of hope. With no other option but to wait, I found myself doing just that. Every moment felt like an eternity.

A Visit Would Be Nice

The day of Andrew's surgery came and went, and I heard nothing except the relentless ticking of the clock. I tried to remain positive, but my hope was beginning to dim. When his message arrived two days later, relief flooded me quickly, followed by a feeling of concern. He said he was still in the hospital because of an infection and he would be there for at least another two days. His next words caused my heart to skip a beat as I read a simple invitation:

A visit would be nice.

We messaged back and forth several times until we agreed I would visit the following day. When morning came, my stomach churned with nerves as I gazed at my reflection in the bathroom mirror. I did my best to cover any remaining bruises with makeup since I wanted to look my best when I walked into his hospital room. I had waited for what seemed like an eternity. What would we say when we finally saw each other? Would this be our final goodbye? I couldn't let my mind run away with me. I had to hold on to any remaining hope I could find.

I arrived at the hospital and nervously made my way to the elevator stationed directly behind the visitor desk. With a trembling finger, I pushed the button for the tenth floor. Navigating the unfamiliar hallways, I reached the nurses' station, where I was kindly directed to Room 1013.

I paused. This was it. The time had finally come.

Gathering my resolve, I straightened the pleats of the black and white dress I had carefully chosen to wear. Summoning a brave smile, I knocked softly and pushed the door open.

There sat Andrew looking back at me from the hospital bed and smiling the most beautiful smile I had ever seen. He was hooked up to an IV and oxygen, and his right arm was heavily bandaged from the top of his shoulder down to his fingertips and firmly fastened to his side with a sling, but he motioned for me to come in.

"Hi," he said with a grin.

"Hi," I replied, my own voice shaking.

The silence that followed was deafening. Before I lost my nerve, I gathered my courage and spoke the words that had weighed so heavily on my heart.

"Andrew, where do we go from here?"

He hesitated before continuing.

"I don't know," he replied. "I've read the police reports and know what happened to you. You know what happened to me. I think we're both going to be messed up."

I couldn't bear to let him continue. Determined to stop him before he said any more, I raised my finger and wagged it in the air. Though my voice trembled with uncertainty, I summoned all the resolve I could find.

"Andrew Haar, you will never meet another woman like me!"

Andrew's laughter echoed softly in the hospital room as he reached for my hand, pulling me close. This was all the invitation I needed, so I climbed onto his hospital bed and rested my head against his chest. For the next several hours, time seemed to stand still. We held each other tight while doctors and nurses came and went from the room, each smiling their approval. A tear slipped down my face. Somehow, deep in my heart, I knew that everything was finally going to be okay.

Trusting God in the Valley

It's easy to trust God when we're on the mountaintop of life and everything seems to be going according to plan. Trusting God when we're down in the valley and going from one disappointment to another is a totally different story. Darkness threatens to close in around us and tells us there is no way out, making it easy to lose sight of God's presence. Yet, it's precisely those moments when we need to firmly grasp hold of God's hand and hang on for dear life, trusting He won't let us fall.

From the day I was assaulted until the day I walked into Andrew's hospital room, I wasn't sure how my story would turn out. What I did know that day in his hospital room was that I had taken the words of my pastor's wife seriously when she admonished me in the most loving way possible not to let Andrew replace God in my heart. I had taken a stand and had made sure Andrew knew I loved him, and I had reminded him of his promise to me. I also had decided that no matter the outcome, I would choose to believe God knew better than I did.

During life's trials, it becomes all too easy to place people, possessions, or positions above our relationship with the Lord, unintentionally turning them into idols. Our happiness becomes dependent on whether the people we care about choose to love us back. Our success becomes measured by whether we acquire the same possessions as those we're comparing ourselves to. We get caught in a trap of allowing our jobs and even our God-given dreams to take center stage in our lives, and we begin to relegate our walk with the Lord to the back burner. And then we wonder why we struggle with our faith.

In Deuteronomy 4:23–24, Moses admonished the Israelites, "Be careful not to forget the covenant of the LORD your God that he made with you; do not make for yourselves an idol in the form of anything the LORD your God has forbidden. For the LORD your God is a consuming fire, a jealous God." God had repeatedly showed His love for the Israelites and wanted their love in return. In the same way, God desires to capture our hearts. He is jealous when we place anyone or anything above our love for Him. He yearns for us to spend time with Him and make our relationship with Him our top priority.

I came to understand this more deeply at a point in my first marriage when I found my walk with the Lord had slipped into a state of complacency. At the time, my husband and I had fallen into some hard times, and it looked like our marriage was going under. Determined to fight for my marriage, I committed to setting my alarm for the wee hours so I could get up and pray early each morning. I'd grab my cup of coffee along with my Bible and journal and wait with great expectancy to hear from the Lord. I'd write down what I believed the Lord was saying to me and then record my thoughts and responses as well.

As time went by, things in my marriage temporarily improved, and I let my morning times with the Lord slip away. My alarm would ring and I'd sense the Lord gently nudging me awake, reminding me it was time for us to meet. But instead of getting up and keeping this priority, I'd ignore the nudging, roll over, and go back to sleep.

One day, I realized something was missing in my walk with the Lord. The closeness I'd once felt was no longer there. Not knowing what else to do, I prayed and asked the Lord what had happened. I couldn't understand why He felt so far away.

"Lord, why don't I hear you like I used to?" My prayer felt more like an accusation.

No sooner had the words left my mouth than I distinctly felt His gentle response in my heart: *"Because you don't seek me like you used to."* At that moment, I knew I had been the one who walked away.

In Jeremiah 29:12–14 we read, "'Then you will call on me and come and pray to me, and I will listen to you. You will seek me and find me when you seek me with all your heart. I will be found by you,' declares the LORD." This passage reminds us that when we wholeheartedly seek God, He listens and responds. It's a powerful invitation to pursue Him with unwavering devotion, knowing that in His presence we find solace and restoration.

Pursuing God with a Whole Heart

Merriam-Webster defines *wholehearted* as "completely and sincerely devoted, determined, or enthusiastic" and "free from all reserve or hesitation."[2] King David eloquently wrote in Psalm

27:8, "My heart has heard you say, 'Come and talk with me.' And my heart responds, 'LORD, I am coming'" (NLT). What a beautiful image of how God invites us to spend time with Him in His loving presence.

I encourage you to take a moment here. Close your eyes and ask yourself: What is my current relationship with God like? When was the last time I spent time in His presence for no other reason than to talk with Him and hear His voice? Has it seemed recently that God is far away?

> There's nowhere you can go that God's presence isn't already there to guide and hold you.

My dear friend, know that God hasn't gone anywhere, and He hasn't left you alone. He's as close as the air that you breathe. Psalm 139 says that God knows everything about you—your thoughts, your actions, and even your whereabouts. His hand is upon you, guiding and supporting you everywhere you go. There's nowhere you can go that His presence isn't already there to guide and hold you.

God's Love Is Without End

In Luke 15:11–32, Jesus tells a powerful story of a father's unconditional love for his son. In this parable, a son impetuously asks his father to give him his inheritance now rather than waiting until after his father dies. The son then squanders every penny of his newfound wealth until he finds himself destitute, living on the streets and eating with pigs in a pigpen. When he reaches the end of his rope, the son remembers his father is a good man who treats even his servants well. Humbled, the son returns home in hopes of serving as one of the hired hands. But to his amazement, his father rushes out to greet him and embraces him with outstretched arms. Instead of reproaching him, his father puts a ring on his hand and a robe on his back and throws a party to welcome him home.

This parable reflects God's never-ending love for us. Just like the father in the story, our heavenly Father is waiting for each and every one of us to come home. His arms are open, and He wants nothing more than to embrace us and shower us with His love and forgiveness.

Right now, you might be thinking, "But I haven't left home or turned my back on God like the prodigal son did." Maybe not, but many of us have felt distant from God, especially when facing tough challenges. We've pulled away from Him when we walked through the valley of discouragement. Your valley of discouragement might include struggles like divorce, miscarriage, or abuse. Or maybe you've endured the loss of a loved one, received a daunting diagnosis, or felt the sting of betrayal by a trusted friend.

Like me, do you ever feel like God has somehow forgotten you? The devil wants you to believe that lie, but let me reassure you that nothing could be further from the truth. Not only has God not forgotten you, but He also wants you to know that your story is far from over. Even in the most trying circumstances, God's plan of redemption for your life remains steadfast and unshakable!

It Will Go Fast

One month after I first entered Andrew's hospital room, I experienced God's redemptive power in my life. What the devil had meant for evil to destroy me, God had turned around and crafted for my good.

As Andrew recuperated and eventually left the hospital, our relationship blossomed in ways we never imagined. It all moved swiftly, but we were both certain we were meant to be together. At our stage in life, we knew what mattered most: us. After four short weeks, Andrew asked for my hand in marriage. It all happened fast, just as God had told me it would! Together, we embarked on a whirlwind journey of wedding planning for the date we set just four months later.

The evening before our wedding, I invited my youngest daughter to spend the night with me. As I lay beside her, memories of the nights following my assault flooded back. Gently, I reached for her hand and, realizing she had already drifted off to sleep, quietly laced my fingers through hers. Contentment filled my heart. The next day I was going to marry the man of my dreams.

My alarm clock went off at 6:30 the next morning. The day I thought might never come was finally here! Jumping out of bed, I ran through a mental list of things I knew still needed to be done. *Had I remembered to give the photographer the correct address? What if the sound person forgot the microphone? Did I have enough decorations? Who would set up the outdoor trellis we planned to stand under during the ceremony?*

Pulling on a T-shirt and jeans, I threw my hair into a ponytail and hurried to begin my day. But as I prepared to leave the house, a sudden realization stopped me in my tracks: There was one last, very important appointment I couldn't miss.

Dancing for an Audience of One

Stashing my cell phone in my purse, I tiptoed out of my bedroom, careful not to disturb my sleeping daughter. My car was ready, packed with everything I would need for the day. But first I headed in the familiar direction of my uncle and aunt's house. When I pulled into their driveway, the hum of my car's engine faded into silence. Making my way to the backyard fence, I unlatched the gate with a gentle click. Tiptoeing past the kitchen windows, I followed the familiar cement path leading to the pergola nestled beneath the trees.

By now the sun was rising, and I could feel its warmth on my face. Closing my eyes, I reverently tilted my face toward heaven and whispered a prayer of thanksgiving. I thanked the Lord for the countless mornings I'd been allowed to spend at the pergola this past summer, finding solace and healing for my wounded heart.

Here, in this sacred space, I had poured out my soul, knowing the Lord would always be here waiting for me.

In the distance, the birds began their morning chorus. I smiled and vowed never to let the busyness of life consume me to the point of forgetting the precious moments spent in communion with God in this hallowed place. For it was here, as I lay face down in my suffering and pain, that I knew God had heard me.

Later that day I would stand before a large audience of friends and commit my life and love to my new husband. But before stepping into that new chapter, I felt compelled to stop and take a moment to honor the One who had taught me the true essence of love. I decided to start this day with a special dance dedicated to my audience of one: God.

The melody from my phone filled the air, setting the stage for my dance beneath the pergola. As I assumed my familiar stance, it felt like countless mornings before. Closing my eyes, I allowed myself to be carried away by the music, feeling as though I was wrapped in a divine embrace, dancing with the Lord.

There was a hush in the air, and all of heaven witnessed my feet twirling around and around as I hummed the tune of "Dance with Me." My anthem. Its familiar melody had accompanied me through countless mornings at the pergola. With each graceful twirl, I surrendered to the rhythm, my heart offering a silent prayer: *Lord, lead me wherever You may, and I promise to trust You enough to follow.*

When the song was over, the music softly faded away and I sensed the moment coming to a close. It was time for me to leave and say a final goodbye to the special pergola that had become a holy place for me to meet with the Lord. The summer had come to an end, and I knew this would be my final dance here. Today marked the beginning of a new chapter, as I would join my husband in our new home and leave behind my summer at the pergola.

With my customary curtsy of reverence, I concluded my dance the way I always had by silently expressing gratitude and surrender to the unseen Partner who had guided and loved me throughout this journey. As I gathered my belongings and prepared to leave, I couldn't resist stealing one last glance over my shoulder.

This place was more than just a concrete dance floor under a pergola; it was a sanctuary of solace and healing. The pergola with its two weathered swings had borne witness to my tears and triumphs, cradling me in its embrace as I navigated through life's highs and lows. The leaves of the trees rustled gently in the breeze and seemed to wrap themselves around me. And as the sun peeked through the branches, casting its golden rays, I felt as though nature itself was bidding me farewell.

With a sense of anticipation, I turned away from this familiar sanctuary, ready to embrace the adventures that awaited me.

Remember Your First Love

One of the most important lessons I learned that summer at the pergola was the importance of keeping my love for the Lord as my top priority. In Revelation 2:4–5, Jesus has words for the church at Ephesus. Their love for Jesus had grown cold and was turning into rules and religiosity. He tells John to deliver this message to them: "But I have this against you, that you have abandoned the love you had at first. Remember therefore from where you have fallen; repent, and do the works you did at first. If not, I will come to you and remove your lampstand from its place, unless you repent" (ESV).

Before the attack, I had found myself in a place much like that of the Ephesian church—spiritually distracted and going through the motions of religion while losing sight of my relationship with Jesus. I had lost focus on my first love. But when life dealt me a devastating blow, I realized how complacent my faith had become.

This new awareness helped me see a truth I hadn't understood before: During difficult times we face a choice—to either let our hardships pull us further from God or let them turn us to Him for strength and guidance. I discovered that even in the midst of pain, God could use my trials to deepen my relationship with Him, moving me from places of spiritual complacency to a deeper, more authentic faith. When I returned my focus to God, I learned to embrace my childlike faith once again and develop a dependency on Him.

You already know what I was experiencing when I began this transformation. But what about you? Do you feel spiritually empty and exhausted from life's battles? Have you forgotten the excitement and passion of your faith? Perhaps you'd like to experience a shift into a deeper faith of your own. If so, God invites you to return to your first love and rediscover the vibrant relationship you once cherished.

With this goal in mind, let's explore five steps for rekindling your love for the Lord. These steps are not just for times of hardship. No matter where you are in your journey, whether you're facing challenges or not, these principles can help you deepen your relationship with God, bring a renewed sense of purpose and passion to your faith, and help you rediscover the joy of walking with Him.

1. **Remember.** Recall what it was like when you first surrendered your heart to Jesus. (If you've never given your heart to Jesus and would like to do so now, refer to the prayer at the end of this chapter.) Think back to the excitement you felt, the eagerness to spend time in prayer and reading God's Word. Consider how practices or habits you embraced back then may have faded over time. Allow yourself to reminisce about the joy of surrendering in praise and worship.

2. **Repent.** Ask God to forgive you for allowing yourself to get spiritually distracted and put other things in the place reserved for Him. Confess the moments when you relied on your own strength rather than trusting in Him to meet your daily needs. Ask God to reignite the fire of your passion you once had for Him.

3. **Regroup.** Maybe it's time to reorder your priorities. Take a close look at what things get in the way of your time with the Lord. Are there habits or commitments that you need to adjust? Perhaps you need to let go of certain things to create space for Him in your life.

4. **Reengage.** Pulling away from the fellowship and community of other believers often causes our faith to grow cold. Remaining connected to like-minded individuals can help keep our faith vibrant and strong, much like the way hot coals maintain their heat when kept together. Consider whether you need to seek out a new community that will provide encouragement and support in your faith journey.

5. **Receive.** It is important that we not only *ask* for God's forgiveness but that we also *receive* His forgiveness. First John 1:9 says, "If we [freely] admit that we have sinned and confess our sins, He is faithful and just [true to His own nature and promises], and will forgive our sins and cleanse us continually from all unrighteousness [our wrongdoing, everything not in conformity with His will and purpose]" (AMP).

By utilizing these five steps, you're not just going through the motions of religious duty. You're actively rekindling your love for God and restoring the vibrant relationship you once had with Him. I pray that as you implement these steps in your own life, you will experience the transformative power of God's love and find renewed strength and joy in your faith journey as I did.

The Dance Continues

During my time at the pergola, my connection with the Lord deepened and my trust in Him grew stronger than ever before. On my wedding day, I said goodbye to my summer pergola meeting place with the Lord, but I knew He would accompany me wherever life led. Together we would create and discover a new special place where the two of us could meet. Recognizing the ease with which complacency can creep into my spiritual journey, I made a commitment to remain vigilant in recognizing warning signs before that happened again.

Secluded in the bridal chamber, filled with anticipation and love, I waited as guests took their seats in the rows of white wooden chairs outside. The trellis where Andrew and I would recite our vows had been covered with flowers and placed on the shore of a lake, setting the stage for a perfect day.

The time came for my dad to enter the room where I had been waiting. Our eyes locked as he walked toward me. Standing in front of me was the very first man I had ever loved. I wrapped my arms around him as tears fell down my cheeks. I buried my face in his chest and for one long moment was held in the arms of my daddy.

This was the man who had stood beside me and witnessed every tear and heartache. This was the man who had encouraged me to make a list of what I wanted to believe God for in a mate. This was the man who had prayed for me and believed God for me, especially when I couldn't.

The music grew louder, signaling it was time for us to go. Andrew would be waiting for me under the trellis. Linking arms with my father on one side and my son on the other, the three of us walked down the aisle and I became Mrs. Andrew Haar.

Our celebration with friends and family continued long into the night. Most of these people had been there to support us and had stood beside us through the hard times we had endured. It seemed only fitting they be a part of celebrating our new life together.

This day had begun with the most important dance of my life, and it ended with a dance in my new husband's arms. We held each other tightly and promised to never again let each other go.

I recognize that not all stories end like mine. You may be reading this right now and saying, "That's great for you, Kim, but what about me?" And I wish I knew all the answers. I wish I could guarantee that everything you've been hoping and waiting for would turn out exactly the way you've prayed, but I can't. I'm only human. What I am certain of is that, whatever your circumstances, God loves you and wants to bring you healing, and He wants to dance with you too. What that dance looks like is for you to discover.

Though I can offer no guarantees, there is One who can. Our heavenly Father's steadfast love never changes. He promises that no matter what comes our way in life, we will never have to face it alone; He will always walk beside us. His love for us will never change, and we can come directly to His throne, where He offers grace for our mistakes and washes us whiter than snow. Best of all, when we bring our desires and dreams to Him and tell Him, "Lord, I trust you," He will say, "Put your feet on mine and watch what I can do!"

PAUSE AND REFLECT

- Reflect on your priorities and examine whether you've allowed anything or anyone to take the place of importance in your heart designed for only God. Have you unknowingly let these things turn into idols that control your happiness? Take time to honestly assess and journal your thoughts, laying them before God in prayer. Ask Him to help you realign your heart and put Him back in His rightful place of importance.

- Consider establishing a dedicated time and space for meeting with the Lord. Whether it's a quiet corner of your home, a secluded place in nature, a special place in your closet, or a cozy nook in your garden, carve out a space where you can retreat from distractions and commune with the Lord. Set aside a specific time each day for this encounter, even if it's just for a few minutes. Practice the art of conversation with God, both speaking and listening in the stillness. Just as nurturing a friendship requires an investment of time, so does deepening your relationship with Jesus. (See "The Power of Place" in Tools for Growth and Healing.)

- If, after reading this chapter, you recognize you have lost the excitement and zeal you once had for the Lord, reread the five steps for rekindling your love for Him: remember, repent, regroup, reengage, and receive. These steps offer a pathway back to the vibrant and intimate relationship you desire with Him.

PRAYER OF OUR HEART

Dear Heavenly Father,

Thank You for loving me before I ever loved You. Thank You for shedding Your blood on the cross so that every broken place of my heart could be mended and healed. I ask You to forgive me for my failings and shortcomings. Take the wounds and scars life has caused me and transform them into a thing of beauty. Remind me to keep You as my priority and to never let other things take Your place in my heart.

Jesus, I believe You died on the cross for me and I confess You as my Lord and Savior. I ask for Your help in areas where I need to trust You with my dreams and with the people I love so much and need to commit to Your care. Ignite my desire to spend time with You and get to know You as the Lord of my life. In Your mighty name I pray. Amen.

Epilogue

A Time to Move On

We are products of our past, but we don't have to be prisoners of it.

RICK WARREN

I used to think I hated the word "strong." For a long time following my assault, people who heard my story would come up to me and say, "You are so strong!" I knew they meant it as a compliment; however, the looks of sympathy accompanying those four simple words only reminded me that I had gone through something horrible and had somehow managed to struggle and find my way out.

However, over time and through the study of God's Word, my opinion of the word "strong" has changed. Throughout the Bible, God repeatedly tells us that He desires us to be strong and to find refuge in Him.

> Be strong and courageous. Do not be afraid or terrified because of them, for the LORD your God goes with you; he will never leave you nor forsake you. (Deut. 31:6)

Have I not commanded you? Be strong and courageous. Do not be afraid; do not be discouraged, for the LORD your God will be with you wherever you go. (Josh. 1:9)

> Be strong and take heart,
>   all you who hope in the LORD. (Ps. 31:24)

> My flesh and my heart may fail,
>   but God is the strength of my heart
>   and my portion forever. (Ps. 73:26)

Be on your guard; stand firm in the faith; be courageous; be strong. (1 Cor. 16:13)

Finally, be strong in the Lord and in his mighty power. (Eph. 6:10)

True strength isn't found in our own abilities but in trusting God's unwavering power. When we do this, He gives us the strength we need.

It has now been seven years since the summer my world fell apart. In quiet moments, I find myself contemplating the valuable insights I gained during this stormy season of my life. While I have no desire to go back and relive any part of that summer, I wouldn't trade anything for the wisdom I acquired through my experience—insights that rekindled my love for God and taught me how to trust Him more deeply and how to dance with Him.

I learned that the struggle is real.

The struggle to hold on to hope when all you can see is loss.

The struggle to surrender when all you want to do is control.

The struggle to forgive when all you feel is anger and hate.

The struggle to heal when you'd rather nurse your wounds.

The struggle to believe when you're plagued with constant doubt.

The struggle to trust God's plan when you'd rather make the plan.

I want to be careful not to leave the wrong impression. Just because I say that I made the decision to trust God doesn't mean it was always easy. My struggles often felt like a tug-of-war. One moment I felt optimistic, as if I was winning my battle with fear and defeat. The next moment I wrestled with the belief that nothing would ever work out and that I should give up.

If you find yourself resonating with these thoughts and emotions, know that you're not alone. It's vital to recognize and validate our feelings. These are real struggles and must be acknowledged. However, we shouldn't let our feelings dictate our actions. That's why immersing ourselves in the Word of God and obeying His teachings are crucial. His promises are always reliable. Allow me to share some of the essential lessons I learned going through adversity.

Key Lessons I Learned Going Through Adversity

1. When you experience adversity, you have a choice to be either defined or refined by what has happened to you.

God wants to refine our lives and remove our impurities much like a refiner does with precious metals. To remove impurities from precious metals, a refiner melts the ore and heats it until all the dross rises to the surface. Before it cools, these impurities are skimmed off until all that's left is the precious metal. The fire doesn't consume or destroy the metal; it just removes the impurities. The end product is more valuable than what they started with.

In my own life, I became aware of impurities God wanted to remove: pride, the need to control, making idols of others, and making myself my own version of God.

Pride fueled my anger and said I didn't deserve what I was going through. In my mind, I had been a good Christian and done everything by the book. I felt God was not keeping His end of the bargain. I believed that if I did everything God wanted, He was obliged to shower me with blessings.

I noticed my tendency to control things when I began dictating to God what I thought was best. This stemmed from a place of thinking I had it all figured out better than He did. Instead of surrendering and leaning on His guidance, I let my self-reliance get in the way.

And when it came to my faith, I realized I had placed too much weight on others for my happiness. I unwittingly prioritized my love for others over my love and devotion to God, turning them into idols in the process.

During this journey, I realized the importance of repentance. I asked God to refine me and remove these impurities from my life so I could serve and rely on Him alone.

2. Seasons change, but they also come again and again.

Like the physical seasons we observe in the natural world, we all go through changing seasons in life. Seasons of weeping and sorrow that seem like they will last forever. Seasons when laughter and joy can feel just out of reach. Seasons of waiting when it seems like nothing is happening. Seasons of disappointment and discouragement when we feel alone. And also seasons of celebration, triumph, and dancing.

Even though it may sometimes feel like a particular season will last forever, it won't. In telling my story, I have tried to be as transparent as possible about my journey through the various seasons of joy, sadness, hope, loss, excitement, discouragement, celebration, and mourning. However, there's a part of my story I haven't fully shared until now. In the tumultuous years leading up to my assault, not only did I discover my ex-husband's infidelity and go through a heart-wrenching divorce that ended my marriage of twenty-three years, but I also journeyed alongside my mother as she received a breast cancer diagnosis that landed her in the ICU, where she slipped into a five-week coma. Seven doctors told us that she would be in a vegetative state for the rest of her life. (Spoiler alert: Just before we were going to take her off life support, my mom woke up and now leads a completely normal life!)

Six months later, my dad was diagnosed with an aggressive form of cancer. Doctors told us he would most likely have a short time to live. (Spoiler alert: He underwent chemotherapy treatment and remains cancer-free to this day almost nine years later.)

Just when it seemed like the worst was behind us, my ex-husband assaulted me, adding another layer of trauma. Have you ever heard the saying "When it rains, it pours"? At times, I felt like a modern-day Job and wondered what new disaster would strike next.

I have come to view life as a roller coaster that takes us on a wild ride. It throws loops, twists, and turns that can make you feel completely out of control. What you *can* control, however, is the decision to cling to Jesus with all your might. When you recognize He's right there beside you, holding your hand, and is not fazed by all the ups and downs, you suddenly realize the ride doesn't seem so scary anymore. He's promised never to let go of your hand, and He means it.

Dear friend, I know those hard seasons can feel like they're swallowing you whole. Instead of letting them devour and destroy you, let them shape you. Let them lead you to the foot of the cross. That's where true healing begins.

3. Healing is a daily choice.

Healing can be a slow, agonizing process. Sometimes it felt like I was taking one step forward and two steps back. There were many days when I didn't feel like I was getting anywhere. I didn't feel like forgiving. I didn't feel like trusting. I didn't feel like getting out of bed. I didn't feel like being around friends. And I sure didn't feel like putting in the effort. But in those moments, I had to remind myself that regardless of how I felt, I still had a choice to make. I could choose to either move forward and heal or stay stuck in the same old rut.

Some mornings I would wake up angry over the very thing I had forgiven the previous day, even though I thought I had dealt with it. That's when I'd remind myself that I had a new opportunity to forgive again. When it comes to forgiveness, what matters most is our willingness and obedience to do what God says. He's constantly nudging us to forgive again and again. He's constantly reminding us to trust Him again and again. By making these practices a part of our daily routine, we find the strength to overcome anything that threatens to hold us back.

Choosing healing isn't just waiting for time to soothe the hurt. It's about being intentional. It's about giving yourself the needed space to grieve, having those raw, honest talks with God about how you feel, and being mindful of what you let into your heart and mind. It's also about refusing to let your past define you. You are not a victim; you are a survivor. So, every single day, make that choice to walk in forgiveness, to walk in freedom. That's how you keep moving forward.

4. God gave us an arsenal of weapons to use against the devil, including rest, thanksgiving, and worship.

When we rest, we take God at His word and trust that He will keep His promises. Rest and worry cannot coexist. When we allow ourselves to worry, we breathe life into our problems. When we rest, we take away the devil's ability to torment us with fear, insecurity, and worry.

When we stop to give thanks and count our blessings, God's promises get bigger, our problems get smaller, and our faith becomes stronger. Something happens when we remind ourselves of all the times God has come through for us in the past. It is like fuel for our faith.

When we lift our voices and hearts to God in worship, we're inviting Him right into the middle of our mess. It's like saying, "God, I trust You with this. Take over." Worship requires us to take our eyes off our circumstances and place our eyes on God.

Worrying changes nothing. Worship changes everything. God gave us worship as His secret weapon of mass destruction.

5. There is freedom in surrender.

I've discovered this profound truth: There's a certain freedom that comes with surrendering to God's plan. From our limited, human perspective, it's easy to get caught up in trying to control every aspect of our lives. But when we truly grasp the concept that God sees the bigger picture, it becomes easier to let go and trust His wisdom.

Looking back, I'm glad I see only a part of His grand design. Had I known the challenges that lay ahead, I might have made different choices, altering the course of my life. But God, in His infinite goodness, had already prepared for every twist and turn.

When we learn to trust God with our future, we are free to enjoy our lives. We no longer have to worry about what the future holds because God is already there ahead of us, with all the answers we haven't even thought to ask. Psalm 139:5 beautifully captures this truth: "You go before me and follow me. You place your hand of blessing on my head" (NLT).

As I sit here on my back patio, thinking about the ways God has blessed me, I can't help but notice I'm wearing the same cozy, soft, brown robe that enveloped me the morning after my assault. On one hand, it seems like a lifetime ago. On the other hand, it feels like only yesterday.

In those challenging days, I felt much like Humpty Dumpty, broken and shattered beyond repair. All the king's horses and all the king's men couldn't put my life back together again. But then I called on the King of Kings Himself. Piece by piece, He tenderly gathered the fragments of my life, carefully mending them into a masterpiece of redemption and restoration. Through His grace, I found wholeness once more.

In the introduction of this book, I stated that most of us ask questions at one time or another.

Why is this happening?

Has God forgotten me?

Does God even care?

Today, I want to declare with unwavering certainty that God not only sees you and cares for you, but He also thinks about you nonstop. His thoughts toward you outnumber the grains of sand. You are not overlooked, and there is no such thing as His "left-over" love. You are His first choice. Hear His voice speaking to you now: "I see you. I hear you. I know you. I choose you—again and again. You are Mine!"

Take a moment to embrace this truth and imagine God speaking your name aloud:

"[Insert your name], you are Mine!"

I'm not sure what season of life you find yourself in right now. Stormy seasons eventually come into every person's life. None of us are exempt. When these storms hit, we have a decision to make: Will we run *to* God or *away* from Him?

I often ask myself, "Am I still clinging tightly to Jesus as if my very survival depended on it?" More than anything, I want my answer to be yes. Just like you, I have to keep my relationship with the Lord intentional. It's an ongoing journey that requires continual effort.

Our relationship with the Lord is much like the dynamic between two dance partners: He takes the lead and we follow. If we fail to prioritize our time with Him, we never learn to trust Him. On the other hand, when we make our relationship with Him a priority, we learn to trust Him and willingly respond to His signals. If He gives a signal we weren't expecting, we surrender our own plan and instead follow His lead—no exceptions.

Learning to trust God finally allowed me to heal.

I invite you to join me as I close with this final prayer. Picture me sitting there next to you, reaching my hand out to hold yours. Together, as sisters in Christ, let's make this our prayer:

Lord, let me hold on to You as tightly as I ever have, never forgetting Your faithfulness. Even in moments when Your presence feels distant, remind me that You are always close beside me. Lord, in the hard times, when I fear I might go under, guide me to seek You and nudge me to listen attentively for Your voice.

Lord, I am learning that when I seek You with all my heart, I will find You. I will find You in the warm sunlight on my face. I will feel You in the gentle breeze that blows around me. I will hear You in the rustling of leaves on the trees, and I will hear You in the words of a song, reminding me that in my chaos, You are there.

I ask You to become the Lord of my life. I willingly surrender my will and plans for my life and ask You to replace them with Yours. Thank You for loving me, seeing me, accepting me, and choosing me to be Your treasured daughter. Today, I receive Your love. In Jesus's name I pray. Amen.

Dear reader, I hope someday soon I get a chance to meet you. Until that day, more than anything, I hope you find the strength to heal, the courage to reclaim your life, and the joy of dancing again after your deepest hurts!

Kimberly Haar

Tools for Growth
and Healing

Welcome to a section created specifically for growth and healing. Whether your wounds are fresh or have lingered for years, this space is for you.

In my practice as a licensed professional counselor and trauma therapist, I've come to recognize that pain comes in many different forms. Contrary to widespread belief, there is no such thing as the "Pain Olympics." Each person's journey is unique, and we all experience things differently. While one individual may be greatly affected by an event and, as a result, have residual, life-altering effects, another person may go through the same experience and come out emotionally unscathed. That's why it's so important not to compare our emotional pain to that of others. Acknowledging our experiences and their lasting effects on us validates our feelings of pain and can be the first step toward healing.

In the upcoming pages, you'll discover a range of powerful tools I personally used on my own path to healing. They are intentionally flexible, so you can choose what resonates with you at any given time. If a particular exercise feels overwhelming, it's perfectly okay to set it aside and return to it when you're ready.

These resources can be revisited as often as needed, allowing you to tailor them to suit your changing needs.

As you explore this section, approach it with an open mind and be willing to experiment with different approaches. It's important to adapt these tools to fit your own experiences and challenges. Reflect on how each tool connects with your current situation.

Ultimately, the goal of this section is to shift your perspective from asking, "Why me?"—a question that often keeps us feeling stuck—to declaring, "What now?" which will begin to launch you forward.

As you embark on this journey, know that you are not alone. May these tools be your companions, guiding your hurting heart on the gentle path toward the healing it is looking for!

During tough times, it's natural to want to be alone and shut out the world. But isolating yourself can make things feel even worse. When you're alone, negative thoughts can creep in: "I'm all alone." "Nobody cares about me." "I don't matter." "No one would miss me if I were gone." "Nobody understands." Do any of these thoughts sound familiar?

In recent years, isolation and loneliness have become a silent epidemic. Yet, God did not design us to be alone. He created us with an innate desire to connect with others. When we shut ourselves off and avoid reaching out for help, we miss out on the support we need. Whether it's due to feeling numb, embarrassed, angry, bitter, or too proud, pushing people away only leaves us more isolated in our struggles. As Christians, we're meant to support each other through difficult times.

Understanding the different types of relationships in our lives can help us combat isolation. Recognizing the varying degrees of friendship is particularly beneficial:

- *Best friends*: Those you can confide in and share your deepest thoughts and feelings with.
- *Close friends*: Supportive and understanding, though perhaps not as intimately connected.
- *Social friends*: Companions who bring enjoyment in shared activities.
- *Acquaintances*: Individuals you know casually without a close bond.

Understanding these distinctions helps you prioritize your relationships, ensuring you have a strong support system in place for both good and challenging times. Use the diagram below to identify who currently belongs in each category of your friendship circles. Are there areas that seem sparse or imbalanced? Circle the friendships you might want to cultivate further or where you'd like to develop new relationships.

By engaging in this exercise and continuously nurturing your relationships, you strengthen your support network and combat isolation. This proactive approach will benefit you in both good times and difficult times, ensuring a strong circle of support.

Identifying and evaluating your friendships is key. Building and maintaining friendships is an ongoing process that enriches your life and provides crucial support, especially during challenging times. However, not all friendships are equally beneficial.

Now that you've mapped out your social circles, let's examine the nature of these relationships. It's essential to recognize the qualities of healthy and supportive friendships versus those that may be toxic and draining. Use the chart below to identify your healthiest friendships and consider if there are any you might need to reconsider or let go of. This evaluation is vital for cultivating a strong, positive support network.

A GOOD FRIEND:	A TOXIC FRIEND:
Accepts you as you are and respects you	Drains you of your energy; is all take and no give
Nurtures and supports you throughout the stages of life	Is negative, critical, and intentionally brings you down
Reenergizes you and inspires you to be a better person	Monopolizes the conversation and only talks about themselves, never asking about you
Is not afraid to speak the truth and challenge you to be your best self	Does not respect your time and effort
Listens, shows up, and puts reciprocal effort into your relationship	Never considers or asks your opinion
Doesn't judge or ridicule you	Is never wrong and places blame on everyone else
Makes time for you	Lacks empathy and can't be happy for others
Encourages you to go for your goals	Only calls you when they need something

Trust your instincts when assessing your friendships. Don't hesitate to distance yourself from toxic influences on your well-being. Remember, it's not just about having friends but having the right kind of friends who uplift and support you.

As you review this chart, reflect on your relationships. Which align with positive qualities? Are there any that exhibit concerning traits? While no friendship is perfect, healthy ones should bring more joy and support than stress or pain. Ask God's help in becoming the kind of friend that blesses and encourages others, embodying the positive qualities outlined here.

For more resources on friendship visit
HealingFromLifesDeepestHurtsBook.com/Resources.

Self-care is a familiar term that we hear often, but what does it actually mean? In our hectic lives, it becomes easy to prioritize everyone else's needs over our own. However, contrary to the belief that self-care is selfish, tending to our personal needs is crucial for maintaining our physical, emotional, mental, and spiritual health. In Mark 12:31 Jesus instructs us to love our neighbor *as* ourselves, not *instead of* ourselves. This becomes especially important after experiencing trauma or loss, as self-care becomes a vital part of our healing journey.

During times of crisis or distress, we often feel drained of energy and joy. The mere thought of self-care can seem overwhelming, with even simple tasks like getting out of bed feeling like major accomplishments. It's precisely during these challenging times that our self-care becomes most crucial.

When energy is low, focus on smaller actions. If going for a walk feels daunting, simply sit outside for a while. Order a healthy meal instead of cooking one yourself. Instead of going all out with makeup and hairstyling, simply brush your teeth, comb your hair, and put on fresh clothes. These small steps can significantly impact the way you feel. Ask yourself, "What do I need right now?" The answer might be as simple as giving yourself permission to cry or carving out some much-needed time alone.

Self-care isn't just for tough times; it's equally important in everyday life. Without being intentional, we can easily become imbalanced and overlook important areas of our well-being. Think of self-care as filling your life's bucket, enabling you to support yourself and others. Regularly assess your self-care practices to ensure your bucket remains full. Consistent self-care reduces your risk of burnout, lowers stress level, enhances resilience, and promotes emotional well-being.

On page 209 you'll find a few self-care ideas for both low- and high-energy days. Begin today by incorporating one or two self-care practices into your routine. Remember, investing in self-care isn't selfish—it's a powerful testament to your self-worth. After all, you can't pour from an empty bucket!

For more self-care ideas visit HealingFromLifesDeepestHurtsBook.com/Resources.

"FILL MY BUCKET" LIST

For No- to Low-Energy Days

- Stay off social media
- Try aromatherapy / essential oils
- Practice self-compassion
- Watch a good movie
- Stay hydrated and drink water
- Go to bed early
- Use a weighted eye pillow
- Snuggle with a pet
- Call a friend
- Eat a healthy snack
- Read a book
- Color a picture
- Use a stress ball
- Stand barefoot in the grass
- Express your feelings to someone
- Stretch and move your body
- Take a nap
- Listen to uplifting music
- Engage in prayer
- Journal your feelings
- Meditate for ten minutes
- Spend time in nature
- Take a shower or bath
- Allow yourself to cry
- Take five deep breaths
- Hug someone you care about
- Read inspirational quotes
- Spend time in sunlight
- Use a weighted blanket
- Count to one hundred

For Medium- to High-Energy Days

- Go for a walk, hike, or run
- Go to the gym
- Practice affirmations in the mirror
- Create and follow a daily routine
- Make a playlist of favorite songs
- Reach out to a mentor or role model
- Schedule breaks during work
- Plant a garden
- Engage in a favorite hobby
- Buy yourself flowers
- Visit a friend
- Cook a healthy meal
- Declutter your space
- Get a manicure/pedicure

Imagine your unexpressed thoughts and emotions as a shaken soda bottle, pressure building inside. When left bottled up, this internal pressure can significantly impact our emotional and physical well-being. Research indicates that writing about our traumatic or painful experiences can be a powerful tool for processing and healing.[1]

While writing things down doesn't change past events, it provides a sanctuary for our most vulnerable emotions. This safe space allows us to freely express ourselves without fear of judgment or repercussions. Here, our deepest fears, regrets, and sorrows find refuge, allowing us to process them with honesty and authenticity.

Journaling offers a private outlet for emotions that may feel too overwhelming or raw to share with others. As we pour our innermost thoughts onto the page, we lighten our emotional load and find solace in acknowledging our pain. By writing about emotions we've been avoiding, we send our brain the message that we matter.

Through the act of writing, we gain clarity on our emotions, identify triggers, and recognize negative thought patterns. It provides additional perspective on our problems, making them more manageable, and frees our minds from the grip of unwelcome, intrusive, and ruminating thoughts.

As a timeless companion on our journey of self-discovery, journaling provides a tangible record of our progress. Looking back on past entries allows us to celebrate our victories, no matter how small, and bear witness to our resilience and strength. We can recognize the obstacles we've overcome and the lessons we've learned along the way.

The beauty of journaling is that there is no right or wrong way to do it. You might pour your heart out in prayers, vent frustrations, express yourself through art, collect inspiring quotes, or document moments of gratitude. The possibilities for self-expression and growth are endless.

The following tips will help you embark on your journaling journey and help create a journaling practice that supports both your personal growth and emotional well-being. Remember, each person's journey of self-discovery through writing is unique. Embrace the process and allow your journal to become a trusted companion in your healing and growth.

For FREE journaling prompts visit
HealingFromLifesDeepestHurtsBook.com/Resources.

Tips to Begin Journaling

- ☐ There is no right or wrong way to journal.
- ☐ Find a journal you look forward to writing in.
- ☐ Be consistent with your writing. Schedule it into your day.
- ☐ Avoid typing your entries and write longhand instead.
- ☐ Choose a pen or colored marker that writes easily.
- ☐ Use a "feelings wheel" to help identify your emotions.
- ☐ Set a timer for fifteen minutes. Write whatever comes to mind.
- ☐ Don't judge yourself. Write/draw whatever feels right to you.
- ☐ Choose an environment free of distractions.
- ☐ Use your journal for stress management.
- ☐ Consider journaling prayers to God expressing how you feel.
- ☐ If you need ideas, use journaling prompts to get started.
- ☐ Journaling doesn't have to be perfect. It is for your eyes only.
- ☐ Don't beat yourself up if you miss a few days.
- ☐ Experiment with different times of the day to journal.
- ☐ If you're artistic, include doodles, pictures, or art collages.
- ☐ Incorporate your favorite song lyrics or inspirational quotes.
- ☐ Don't give up. It takes time to form a habit!

As a therapist, I am often asked, "How do I know if therapy is right for me?" My answer is always the same: Everyone can benefit from therapy. Contrary to outdated beliefs, seeking therapy is a sign of strength and resilience, not weakness.

Therapy provides a safe environment where individuals engage in discussions with licensed mental health professionals. These professionals maintain confidentiality (barring threats of self-harm or harm to others), and offer guidance on addressing problematic behaviors, beliefs, and relationships. Therapists also assist in identifying areas for change and growth.

Seeking therapy when struggling with emotional pain is an act of self-care that has multiple benefits. It offers a confidential space to express and explore challenging emotions under an impartial expert's guidance. Therapists provide compassionate support and insight, helping navigate difficult circumstances with empathy and perspective. Therapy equips individuals with practical coping strategies to break free from old patterns, cultivate healthier habits, and forge meaningful connections. Whether navigating a significant life transition, mourning the loss of a loved one, or working through other traumatic events, therapy offers a compassionate place to grieve, heal, and find meaning in the midst of pain.

It is important to recognize that therapy is not exclusively reserved for those in acute distress. In fact, therapy benefits individuals across a wide spectrum of experiences and life circumstances. You don't need to be in crisis or severe pain to seek out therapy; rather, therapy offers valuable support and guidance for anyone seeking personal growth, self-discovery, or enhanced well-being. No issue is too big or small for therapy. If a matter is important to you, it deserves your attention.

Many Christians ask, "What does God think about therapy?" The Bible assures us, "Where there is no guidance, a people falls, but in an abundance of counselors there is safety" (Prov. 11:14

ESV). Receiving counsel is not only a good idea; it's a God idea. Faith and therapy are not mutually exclusive.

As you contemplate seeking therapy, reflect on your goals, readiness for change, and desired outcomes. Prayerfully ask the Lord to lead you to a counselor who honors your faith and integrates biblical truths into the therapeutic process.

Helpful resources for locating a Christian counselor in an area near you include:

American Association of Christian Counselors (aacc.net)

New Life Counselor Network (NewLife.com/counselors/)

Focus on the Family (FocusOnTheFamily.com)

Since navigating therapy for the first time can feel intimidating, the following pages offer answers to frequently asked questions regarding therapy.

Questions About Therapy

How do I choose a good therapist?

Look for a therapist who has expertise in the issues you want to address. Most therapists list their areas of expertise on professional websites. It is acceptable to ask a therapist if they offer a free initial consultation to help you determine if they will be a good fit for your needs. Consider asking trusted friends or family members who have attended therapy for recommendations. Your primary care provider or church leaders may also provide referrals. Online referral sites to consider include aacc.net, NewLife.com, FocusOnTheFamily.com, and PsychologyToday.com.

What is the difference between going to a licensed therapist and a pastoral counselor?

Credentials: Licensed therapists have formal psychology education and are state licensed; pastoral counselors often have religious training but aren't usually state licensed and have less formal oversight.

Religious focus: Pastoral counselors incorporate faith explicitly, while licensed therapists may or may not, depending on client preference.

Scope: Licensed therapists can diagnose mental health disorders; pastoral counselors focus on spiritual guidance and life issues.

Insurance: Licensed therapist services are often covered by insurance; pastoral counseling usually isn't.

How can therapy help me?

Therapy can provide a fresh perspective on your problems, offer emotional support, point you in the right direction of a solution, help you gain healthier coping skills, promote personal growth, help improve your relationships, manage mental health, and support you through life transitions. Therapy empowers you to lead a more balanced, fulfilling life.

Questions About Therapy

What happens during the first therapy session?

The first session is intended to gather basic information, go over consent forms, and discuss your therapeutic goals. It is a chance for you and your therapist to get to know one another. It is totally normal to feel apprehensive about your initial meeting, especially if you've never been to therapy before.

Is therapy expensive?

Therapy costs can vary significantly depending on location, therapist experience, and type of treatment. Here's what to consider:

Rates: Therapist fees differ widely between states and even within cities.

Sliding scales: Some therapists offer reduced rates based on income.

Trainee options: Consider seeing a supervised therapist-in-training for lower costs.

Insurance: If you have health insurance, check your mental health benefits. Ask about deductibles, number of approved sessions, coverage amount per session, and out-of-pocket costs.

For low-cost alternatives, look into community mental health centers or university clinics.

How can therapy help me?

There is no "right" length of time to be in therapy. For most people, there will come a time when therapy no longer feels necessary and you have either reached the goals you established or progress has stalled. In most cases, it is the client who chooses when to end therapy. There are situations when a therapist decides to end sessions and refers a client elsewhere.

Gratitude can sometimes get reduced to cliché slogans like "Have an attitude of gratitude." While it's easy to quickly rattle off a list of things we've come to appreciate, true gratitude goes much deeper. It's about cultivating a mindset that recognizes and values the goodness in our lives and has tangible effects on our well-being.

Cultivating gratitude stimulates serotonin levels in the brain, leading to the production of dopamine, the feel-good chemical. It increases life satisfaction, improves sleep quality, boosts self-esteem, strengthens the immune system, and reduces anxiety and depression. Gratitude also enhances relationships, shifts negative thought patterns, and calms our nervous system.

Training ourselves to have a grateful outlook takes practice. It requires effort, especially in the midst of difficult life circumstances. It's natural to focus on the obstacles and disappointments, but it's crucial to look for and acknowledge the things that are going right in our lives. Through intentional practice, we can retrain our brains to notice and focus on the positive rather than spiraling into discouragement and despair. What you repeatedly bring your attention to becomes stronger over time.

While it's easy to be thankful for the big things that grab our attention, the small, everyday joys often go unnoticed: sunlight streaming through a window, changing colors of autumn leaves, a bird singing in a nearby tree, a blanket to snuggle under on a cold day, or the laughter of children playing. Likewise, we may fail to express appreciation to the people we love assuming they already know how we feel. By voicing our gratitude, we not only uplift others but also deepen our own sense of connection and fulfillment.

Comparison, envy, and unforgiveness are common barriers to gratitude. When we measure our lives against the lives of others or hold on to negative emotions, we risk undermining our contentment and joy. To counteract these obstacles, it's essential to cultivate an intentional gratitude practice.

Ultimately, gratitude is a deliberate choice that shifts our perspective and empowers us to find joy and fulfillment in life's everyday moments. Use the prompts on the next page to remind yourself of the good in your life. Remember—what you focus on, you will invariably find!

For more gratitude resources visit
HealingFromLifesDeepestHurtsBook.com/Resources.

I Am Grateful

**FIVE THINGS
I DID RIGHT
TODAY:**

_____
_____
_____
_____
_____

**WHAT I AM
THANKFUL
FOR TODAY:**

_____
_____
_____
_____
_____

**PEOPLE I AM
GRATEFUL
FOR TODAY:**

_____
_____
_____
_____
_____

**BEAUTY I
EXPERIENCED
TODAY:**

_____
_____
_____
_____
_____

**FIVE WAYS I
HELPED
OTHERS
TODAY:**

_____
_____
_____
_____
_____

We've all been hurt by the words or actions of others. Whether the offense was big or small, intentional or not, wounds can pierce our hearts and leave us with anger, resentment, and bitterness. When we allow our negative feelings to fester, we are the ones who suffer. Unforgiveness impacts not only our physical bodies but also our emotional and spiritual well-being. If left unaddressed, bitterness and resentment can spread like wildfire, often leading to a destructive desire for revenge.

Forgiveness is a deliberate choice, an act of our will. It involves deciding to let go of anger and resentment and adopting a mindset that says, "You don't owe me anything anymore. I am no longer keeping score." Forgiveness isn't based on our feelings but on obedience to God's Word. It's a powerful decision that brings healing and peace, freeing us from the chains of past hurts.

God's Word tells us to bless those who persecute us, *not* to blame them. While our human nature wants to blame, point fingers, hurt, and get even with those who have done us wrong, God's Word tells us to pray they will be blessed. God loves us so much and knows that when we forgive, we are the ones who are set free.

Forgiveness is not the same as reconciliation. While reconciliation can happen, it is not always possible or healthy. Sometimes it's healthier to set a boundary that says, "I forgive you; however, I can no longer have a relationship with you." Forgiveness takes back the power you gave to the one who hurt you.

Other times reconciliation may be unattainable include situations where the offender refuses to communicate or has passed away. Forgiveness doesn't necessitate participation from both parties though. You can forgive someone who isn't sorry and hasn't asked for forgiveness. That's the beauty of forgiveness—you are the one in control of it.

Forgiveness is not always easy. If you find yourself struggling to offer forgiveness, understand that it's a process. Begin by asking

God to soften your heart. Tell Him you desire to forgive but aren't there yet. Being honest with God and yourself is the first step.

It may help to process your feelings in a journal or talk with a pastor or professional who can offer guidance. Be aware that you may never feel "ready" to forgive. That's why forgiveness is a decision and not a feeling. It's a process you might need to revisit again and again, forgiving the same person for the same offense each time something reminds you of the hurt.

If you are wondering, "Where do I begin?" you're already on your journey toward healing. Forgiveness begins with a willingness to even consider the idea of forgiving someone. That is followed by making the decision to forgive. Each time you're reminded of the pain others inflicted, don't allow your mind to ruminate on the offense. Instead, remind yourself of your choice to forgive and ask God for His help. In the beginning, you may need to remind yourself of this time and again. Remember, forgiveness is not a onetime process. It is an ongoing commitment that takes practice.

Extending forgiveness to yourself and others will help you reclaim peace, live in the present, and strengthen your walk with the Lord. Two of the most powerful words you will ever say are "I forgive."

The following pages offer thoughtfully composed prayers on forgiveness. These are designed to support your journey toward healing and making peace with others and yourself. One prayer is for seeking God's help when you're struggling to forgive others, and another is to help you forgive yourself. Use these prayers as a starting point to spark your conversation with the Lord. Feel free to adapt these prayers, adding your own words or changing them to better reflect your personal experiences and feelings.

For additional resources on forgiveness, please visit HealingFromLifesDeepestHurtsBook.com/resources.

Prayer of Forgiveness

A PRAYER TO FORGIVE OTHERS:

Heavenly Father,

I know You see what's in my heart, and right now I'm struggling to forgive. You say in Your Word that we should forgive and even pray for those who hurt us. But honestly, God, I'm struggling with this.

Today, I make the choice to surrender my will and ask You to help me see the ones who hurt me in the same manner that You see them.

Grant me the strength to feel compassion, even when it seems impossible. Help me release the pain I've been carrying and teach me to forgive others as freely as You've forgiven me.

Today, I choose to release (insert name here) from the wrongs that were done to me. Thank You, Lord, for continuing to heal my heart.

In Jesus's name I pray. Amen.

Prayer of Forgiveness

A PRAYER TO FORGIVE MYSELF:

Heavenly Father,

Your Word promises that when we confess our sins, You are faithful and just to forgive us and cleanse us from all unrighteousness. With this assurance, I come before You, asking forgiveness for (fill in the blank).

Lord, help me learn to forgive myself as You have forgiven me. I've been burdened by shame and believed the lie that I'm unworthy of Your love.

Thank You for Your cleansing forgiveness that washes me whiter than snow. Because of Your grace, I can now forgive myself and release the weight of my past mistakes.

Grant me the wisdom and courage to make amends where needed. Guide me in Your truth, teach me Your ways, and lead me on the path of righteousness.

In Jesus's name I pray. Amen.

Music is known for its healing power, and science continues to confirm its profound impact on our brains. It has been said that music uses more parts of the brain than any other function we perform. Studies show that music can help with depression and trauma by calming the body and mind.[2] But music does more than just calm us physically. It also affects us emotionally and mentally. It can evoke memories, stir emotions, and provide a means of expression when words alone fail.

Think about how different types of music influence us. Upbeat songs motivate us in the gym, while tranquil and contemplative songs create a reverent atmosphere in church that helps us connect with God. Whether you resonate with the energetic beats of the gym or the serene melodies of the church, it's undeniable that music deeply shapes our thoughts and feelings.

During tough times, the words we hear matter. Just like music can uplift and heal, it can also offer comfort and strength in times of despair. Connecting with songs of hope, healing, and faith can replenish our spirits and renew our faith. Zephaniah 3:17 reminds us of this: "For the LORD your God is living among you. He is a mighty savior. He will take delight in you with gladness. With his love, he will calm all your fears. He will rejoice over you with joyful songs" (NLT).

No truer words were written about the importance and influence of music than the hymn "Wonderful Words of Life" penned by Philip P. Bliss:

> Sing them over again to me,
> Wonderful words of life;
> Let me more of their beauty see,
> Wonderful words of life.

Words of life and beauty
Teach me faith and duty
Beautiful words, wonderful words,
Wonderful words of life.[3]

Song lyrics have a remarkable ability to infuse life and hope into our hearts. They can uplift our spirits, inspire courage, and offer comfort when times are tough. It's important to be mindful of the music we allow to permeate our minds and souls, as the words we absorb can profoundly impact our thoughts, emotions, and overall well-being. By choosing songs with uplifting and positive messages, we nourish our inner selves and cultivate an attitude of resilience, faith, and optimism.

I put together a "Playlist from the Pergola" with songs that strengthened my faith during difficult times. This collection serves as a wellspring of inspiration and is designed to uplift your spirit and deepen your trust in the Lord when you face challenges.

While this playlist has been meaningful to me, I encourage you to create your own personalized collection. Carefully select songs that resonate with your unique journey, uplift your spirit, and reinforce your faith. Choose melodies and lyrics that remind you of God's unwavering presence and love. Your custom playlist will become a powerful tool of encouragement and strength for you to revisit whenever you need it.

Playlist from the Pergola

Music can be a powerful part of the healing journey. Song lyrics can speak so deeply to the wounds we carry in our hearts. Here are some songs that ministered to me on my own journey.

Praise You in the Storm
Casting Crowns

Even When It Hurts
Hillsong United

Broken Vessels
Hillsong Worship

I Surrender
Hillsong Worship

Just Be Held
Casting Crowns

Worn
Tenth Avenue North

Give Me Faith
Elevation Music

Trust in You
Lauren Daigle

Hold My Heart
Tenth Avenue North

Jesus Hold Me Now
Casting Crowns

Hold Me Jesus
Rich Mullins

Because He Lives
Nicole C. Mullen

Beautiful Things
Gungor

Please Be My Strength
Gungor

God Will Make a Way
Don Moen

Dance with Me
Paul Wilbur

I Am Not Alone
Kari Jobe

Still
Hillary Scott & the Scott Family

Glorious Ruins
Hillsong Worship

Oh, My Soul
Casting Crowns

I Won't Let You Go
Switchfoot

Gentle Healer
Selah

Scan the QR code
for the full playlist!

Like any other meaningful relationship, developing a relationship with the Lord takes time, intentionality, and consistency. When we spend quality time with Him, we learn who He is, what His character is like, and how to hear and distinguish His voice inside us.

It's crucial to understand that God meets us wherever we are. Whether it's a secluded room, a serene spot in nature, or a quiet corner in your home, what matters most is setting aside time to commune with Him.

That said, it can be helpful to have a designated time and place in which we can look forward to meeting with the Lord. This could be a traditional prayer setting, a prayer walk in nature, or even during your daily commute.

Do you have a special place where you meet with God? A place where you can pour out your heart, share your struggles, and worship in silence? Having a routine you anticipate can help you prioritize your spiritual connection amid life's busyness. It doesn't have to be elaborate—the importance lies in consistency and intentionally setting aside time for God.

If you feel any sense of shame as you read this or tell yourself that you are unworthy to meet with the Lord, remember that God's love for you is unshakable. He can't wait for you to come and talk with Him just as you are!

On the following page is a sample guide with ideas for creating a dedicated place for prayer and reflection inside your home. Use these suggestions as inspiration to create a personal sanctuary that nurtures your soul and deepens your relationship with the Lord.

Download additional ideas for creating a sacred place to meet with the Lord in nature or by incorporating a prayer journal at HealingFromLifesDeepestHurtsBook.com/Resources.

CREATING A SACRED PLACE TO
MEET WITH THE LORD

A Special Place Inside Your Home

- Designate a specific area for prayer and biblical meditation, even if it's just a corner.

- Ensure the space is free from distractions to maintain focus during your quiet time.

- Make the area inviting with a comfortable chair, pillows, or a soft blanket.

- Choose lighting that suits your needs—bright for alertness or soft for a calming atmosphere.

- Add meaningful symbols like a cross, Scripture verse, or inspirational picture.

- Keep a Bible and journal readily available in this space.

- Display prayer cards with key Scriptures and photos of people you want to pray for.

- Consider incorporating soft, worshipful music to create a spiritual atmosphere.

- Maintain a journal of answered prayers to encourage your faith.

- Remember this is your personal sacred space—customize it to suit your preferences and needs.

Self-talk is the voice inside our head that influences how we feel about ourselves and the world around us. Just as the Bible instructs us to build ourselves up in the Lord (Jude 1:20), our self-talk can either strengthen and encourage us or tear us down. The words we speak to ourselves hold tremendous power, shaping our perceptions and beliefs. As God's precious children (1 John 3:1), we have the privilege and responsibility to speak life and truth into our lives through our self-talk.

Our self-talk is often shaped by early life experiences and the messages we received from others. Negative beliefs formed in childhood can persist into adulthood, affecting our self-esteem and self-worth. However, as God's children, we are called to renew our minds and align our thoughts with His truth (Rom. 12:2). By recognizing and challenging negative self-talk, we can begin to change our internal dialogue and cultivate a more positive mindset rooted in God's love and His promises.

Positive self-talk encourages us to embrace our identity as beloved children of God and to view ourselves through His eyes. It reminds us of our worth and purpose, and encourages us to embrace our strengths, try new things, and show ourselves compassion.

On the other hand, negative self-talk undermines our sense of self-worth and is much like an internal bully that breeds feelings of self-doubt, anxiety, and inadequacy. It magnifies our flaws and makes us feel disempowered. It is vital that we guard our hearts and minds against destructive self-talk and instead speak life-affirming truths.

Changing self-talk begins with recognizing our negative thought patterns and challenging them with more compassionate and realistic messages rooted in Scripture. We can replace negative statements with affirmations that reflect God's love, grace, and power at work within us. By intentionally filling our minds with God's truth and declaring His promises over our lives, we can transform our self-talk from a source of shame and discouragement to a source of strength and encouragement.

Strategies to learn to change the way we think and talk to ourselves include:

Recognize your internal bully voice. Listen to how you speak to yourself when no one else is listening.

Reframe the message you tell yourself. Use a gentler, kinder attitude when speaking to yourself. Instead of condemning yourself with words like "I'm a failure," try telling yourself, "I didn't succeed at this, but I am really proud of myself for trying!"

Refocus your self-talk to be positive. Begin each day with a positive affirmation as you look in the mirror. Smile at yourself. Speak to yourself as you would speak to a friend.

Realign your thoughts with what God says about you. When you criticize yourself, you are criticizing God since He's the one who made you. Remember that when God sees you, He sees His reflection!

Implementing these strategies can cultivate a mindset of resilience, faith, and empowerment, enabling us to navigate life's challenges with confidence and grace.

Using the following page as an example, begin confronting your negative self-talk and embracing a perspective that aligns with the way God sees you. By consistently affirming yourself with positive words, you'll gradually internalize these truths.

For additional resources on self-talk, please visit HealingFromLifesDeepestHurtsBook.com/Resources.

When I Say . . . God Says

WHEN I SAY: "I'm worthless!"

GOD SAYS: **"You were bought with a price!" (1 Cor. 6:20)**

WHEN I SAY: "I was a mistake!"

GOD SAYS: **"I planned you before you were born!" (Jer. 1:5)**

WHEN I SAY: "I can't go on!"

GOD SAYS: **"My grace is sufficient!" (2 Cor. 12:9)**

WHEN I SAY:

GOD SAYS:

WHEN I SAY:

GOD SAYS:

WHEN I SAY:

GOD SAYS:

WHEN I SAY:

GOD SAYS:

WHEN I SAY:

GOD SAYS:

WHEN I SAY:

GOD SAYS:

WHEN I SAY:

GOD SAYS:

Simply stated, prayer is an open dialogue with God. It is a sacred conversation with the Creator of the universe and a space where we can freely share our deepest thoughts and feelings.

One of the most beautiful things about prayer is that anyone can do it, regardless of background, status, or circumstance. There are no prerequisites, qualifications, or criteria to meet. God simply desires the sincerity of our hearts and invites us to come just as we are.

Many individuals allow preconceived notions and misconceptions to hinder their sense of worthiness in prayer. They feel pressured to articulate perfect words and worry that their prayers won't be eloquent enough for God to hear. Nothing could be further from the truth! Prayer is not about reciting specific words; in fact, there are no perfect words needed for prayer. It consists of simple, heartfelt expressions that anyone can say. It's just talking to the Lord. Merely whispering the name "Jesus" is a complete prayer in itself. "Lord, I need your help" is a complete prayer. Every prayer, no matter how imperfect, holds significance in God's eyes.

There are many therapeutic benefits of prayer. It soothes our souls in the midst of challenges, alleviates stress, calms fear, and reduces loneliness, anxiety, anger, and depression. Prayer also makes a person more inclined to forgive.

When going through hard times, prayer provides a safe place to express all our emotions openly. We can voice our doubts, fears, and insecurities without fear of reproof. Sensing God's presence brings comfort and reminds us we are not alone. It reassures us that our struggles are seen and understood.

But prayer isn't just about asking for things. It's also about spending time in God's presence, receiving His unconditional love and acceptance. Just as we come to know other people by being in relationship with them, we come to know God by spending time with Him. We do this through prayer, quiet moments of reflection, whispered words of thanks, and heartfelt requests for guidance.

Studies have shown that how a person views the character of God determines the effects of prayer on their mental health.[4] A person who prays to a loving and protective God is less likely to experience anxiety-related disorders compared with a person who doubts God will be there for them and prays without expecting to receive comfort or protection. It's vital therefore that we understand the true nature and character of God.

Scripture describes God as all-wise, all-knowing, and all-powerful. According to Psalm 139:1–4, God knows us better than we know ourselves. He is also a loving and forgiving Father who adopts us as His children and always keeps His promises (see Lam. 3:22–23; Rom. 8:15; Heb. 10:23; 1 John 1:9).

If you feel lost and don't know where to start, just say the name "Jesus." Be real with God, pouring out your doubts, fears, anger, and struggles. Speak to Him honestly and openly, without holding anything back, about how hard it is for you to trust Him. If your heart is heavy and you have no words to say, let your tears speak for you. If music resonates with you, let the lyrics of a worship song express the deepest cries of your heart to God.

Remember that prayer is not about perfection but about connection with our heavenly Father. So let's embrace the gift of prayer, knowing that it has the power to heal, comfort, and change us from the inside out. God is waiting to hear from us!

The following pages are packed with Bible verses that are God's promises to us. As you read through the verses, find those that fit your situation and start praying those words confidently. Praying God's promises will boost your faith and push fear aside because faith and fear cannot coexist. Let these verses be your source of strength and confidence on your healing journey.

Download a free copy of "100 Promises from God's Word" at HealingFromLifesDeepestHurtsBook.com/Resources.

Promises from God's Word

1. God will never leave me nor forsake me. (Heb. 13:5)
2. The Lord will fight for me. (Exod. 14:14)
3. God is with me in trouble. (Ps. 91:15)
4. Great shall be the peace of my children. (Isa. 54:13)
5. God will supply all my needs. (Phil. 4:19)
6. God works all things for my good. (Rom. 8:28)
7. Nothing can separate me from God's love. (Rom. 8:38)
8. God will make my path straight. (Prov. 3:6)
9. I am a new creation in Christ. (2 Cor. 5:17)
10. God is able to keep me from falling. (Jude 1:24)
11. God hears my prayers. (Jer. 29:12)
12. God has plans for my future. (Jer. 29:11)
13. God will prosper the work of my hands. (Ps. 1:3)
14. God watches over me while I sleep. (Ps. 4:8)
15. Even before I call, God hears me. (Isa. 65:24)
16. God will deliver me. (Ps. 18:2)
17. God is with me wherever I go. (Josh. 1:9)
18. God gives me a sound mind. (2 Tim. 1:7)
19. God will protect me from deadly disease. (Ps. 91:3)
20. God is my sure anchor. (Heb. 6:19)
21. God will turn my ashes into beauty. (Isa. 61:3)
22. God will give me rest. (Matt. 11:28)
23. God gives His angels charge over me. (Ps. 91:11)
24. God forgives me of my sin. (1 John 1:9)
25. God has given me eternal life with Him. (Rom. 6:23)

Promises from God's Word

26. God renews my strength. (Isa. 40:31)
27. God is my rock. (Ps. 18:2)
28. I have been anointed by God. (1 John 2:20)
29. God goes before me. (Deut. 1:30)
30. God will fulfill His promises for me. (Ps. 138:8)
31. When I am afraid, I can trust in God. (Ps. 56:3)
32. God knows my name. (Isa. 43:1)
33. God rejoices over me with singing. (Zeph. 3:17)
34. God treasures me. (Deut. 26:18)
35. By Jesus's wounds, I am healed. (Isa. 53:5)
36. God calls me His friend. (John 15:15)
37. God keeps His word. (1 Kings 8:56)
38. God will rescue me. (Ps. 91:14)
39. God will complete His work in me. (Phil. 1:6)
40. God daily carries me in His arms. (Ps. 68:19)
41. God will restore and establish me. (1 Pet. 5:10)
42. God is a covenant keeper. (Deut. 7:9)
43. God is good. (Ps. 136:1)
44. God will give me wisdom. (James 1:5)
45. I will reap a harvest if I don't give up. (Gal. 6:9)
46. God is doing something new inside me. (Isa. 43:18–19)
47. God answers me when I call. (Jer. 33:3)
48. God's peace guards my mind. (Phil. 4:6–7)
49. God is close to me in my sadness. (Ps. 34:18)
50. God's goodness and mercy follow me. (Ps. 23:6)

For additional resources to complement the Tools for Growth and Healing, visit HealingFromLifesDeepestHurtsBook.com /Resources or KimberlyHaar.com/Resources.

I encourage you to share your own healing journey with others. Post photos, meaningful passages, and reflections related to this book on social media using these hashtags:

#HealingFromLifesDeepestHurtsBook
#KimberlyHaar

For ongoing encouragement, subscribe to my free "Words of Hope" newsletter at KimberlyHaar.com.

Acknowledgments

This book is dedicated to my incredible family and friends, who stood by me during the most difficult moments of my life. First and foremost, thank you to my parents. From the time I was little, you instilled in me the unwavering belief that God is good and trustworthy. You have been my anchor in life's storms. Thank you for holding me close when I needed to cry and for steadfastly guiding me with your wisdom and faith.

To my children: You are the greatest treasure of my life. Your love and fierce protection kept me going when I felt like giving up. Your courage to support me as I share my story fills me with admiration. You are truly some of the bravest souls I know.

I will forever be indebted to the remarkable and talented women who cheered me on and helped bring this book into the world. Suzie Eller, Kim Spence, Sarah Farrish, and Lisa Whittle, your encouragement, support, and guidance have been invaluable every step of the way. I am profoundly grateful for each of you.

Lastly, to my beloved husband, Andrew. You were well worth the wait! You are by far the most incredible man I have ever known. I have never felt more cherished and celebrated than I do when I am with you. You are my forever perfect dance partner, inspiring me to be the best version of myself. Here's to the countless dances we have yet to share and the bright future ahead of us. I believe with all my heart that our best days are yet to come!

Notes

Chapter 1 A Time to Be Born

1. Strong's Greek Lexicon (KJV), s.v. "G3813 *paidion*," Blue Letter Bible, accessed December 27, 2023, https://www.blueletterbible.org/lexicon/g3813/kjv/tr/ss1/0-1.

Chapter 2 A Time to Let Go

1. Henry Cloud, *Necessary Endings: The Employees, Businesses, and Relationships That All of Us Have to Give Up in Order to Move Forward* (New York: HarperCollins, 2011), 66.

2. Merriam-Webster Dictionary, s.v. "devour," accessed July 18, 2022, https://www.merriam-webster.com/thesaurus/devour.

3. Merriam-Webster Dictionary, s.v. "sham (v.)," accessed July 18, 2022, https://www.merriam-webster.com/dictionary/sham.

4. *The Wizard of Oz*, directed by Victor Fleming (Burbank, CA: Warner Bros. Pictures, 1939; 1996), DVD, scene 23.

5. Darran Simon, "Tour of Grief Is Over for Killer Whale No Longer Carrying Dead Calf," CNN, August 12, 2018, https://www.cnn.com/2018/08/12/us/orca-whale-not-carrying-dead-baby-trnd/index.html.

6. "T.D. Jakes Sermons: Nothing Just Happens," YouTube video, 10:27, February 9, 2014, https://www.youtube.com/watch?v=A6224mKoiww.

Chapter 3 A Time to Laugh

1. Norman Cousins, "Anatomy of an Illness (as Perceived by the Patient)," *New England Journal of Medicine* 295, no. 26 (1976): 1458–63.

Chapter 4 A Time to Hope

1. Strong's Greek Lexicon (KJV), s.v. "G1680 *elpis*," Blue Letter Bible, accessed December 27, 2023, https://www.blueletterbible.org/lexicon/g1680/kjv/mgnt/0-1/.

Chapter 5 A Time to Weep

1. Nightbirde, "Bald Girl in the Dark," October 30, 2020, https://www.nightbirde.co/blog/2020/10/30/bald-girl-in-the-dark.

Chapter 6 A Time to Heal

1. Kellie Johnson, "The Gift of Grief," in(courage), October 2, 2019, https://www.incourage.me/2019/10/the-gift-of-grief.html.
2. Facebook direct message to author, August 10, 2013.
3. Quoted in *The Goal and the Glory: Christian Athletes Share Their Inspiring Stories*, compiled by Josh Davis, (Ventura, CA: Regal, 2008), 130.

Chapter 7 A Time to Trust

1. Watty Piper, *The Little Engine That Could* (New York: Grosset & Dunlap, 1930).
2. *Ellicott's Commentary for English Readers*, s.v. "Proverbs 16:3," Bible Hub, accessed August 5, 2022, https://biblehub.com/commentaries/ellicott/proverbs/16.htm.
3. *Willy Wonka & the Chocolate Factory*, directed by Mel Stuart (Los Angeles: Paramount Pictures, 1971).
4. Facebook direct message to author, May 9, 2017.

Chapter 8 A Time to Forgive

1. Anne Lamott, *Traveling Mercies: Some Thoughts on Faith* (New York: Anchor Books, 1999), 134.
2. Phillips, Craig & Dean, "Tell Your Heart to Beat Again," YouTube video, March 24, 2022, https://www.youtube.com/watch?v=iGVUwDiHKLU.

Chapter 9 A Time to Dance

1. Kelly Richman-Abdou, "Kintsugi: The Centuries-Old Art of Repairing Broken Pottery with Gold," My Modern Met, March 5, 2022, https://mymodernmet.com/kintsugi-kintsukuroi/.
2. Merriam-Webster, s.v. "wholehearted," accessed December 20, 2023, https://www.merriam-webster.com/dictionary/wholehearted.

Tools for Growth and Healing

1. Karen A. Baikie and Kay Wilhelm, "Emotional and Physical Health Benefits of Expressive Writing," *Advances in Psychiatric Treatment* 11, no. 5 (2005): 338–46, doi:10.1192/apt.11.5.338.
2. Fátima Reynolds, "The Transformative Power of Music in Mental Well-Being," American Psychiatric Association, August 1, 2023, https://www.psychiatry.org/news-room/apa-blogs/power-of-music-in-mental-well-being.
3. Philip P. Bliss, "Wonderful Words of Life" (1874), public domain, https://hymnary.org/text/sing_them_over_again_to_me_wonderful.
4. "New Study Examines the Effects of Prayer on Mental Health," PsychCentral, last updated September 18, 2014, https://psychcentral.com/blog/new-study-examines-the-effects-of-prayer-on-mental-health#1.

KIMBERLY HAAR is a licensed therapist, writer, speaker, podcaster, and guest cohost on network radio. She has dedicated her life to empowering others to embrace their true identity and purpose. With over seventeen years of experience in her counseling practice, she has become a trusted guide for those seeking hope and healing.

In addition to her counseling expertise, Kimberly cohosts the podcast *Keepin' It Real!* and frequently serves as a guest cohost on the Oasis Radio Network, where she engages in candid conversations about life, faith, and everything in between. Beyond her professional achievements, her greatest joys are her roles as wife, mom, proud grandma, and follower of Jesus.

Grounded in grit and guided by God's Word, Kimberly's passion lies in helping women break free from the things that hold them back and step into the abundant life that awaits them. Drawing from her own experience of overcoming adversity, she inspires others to shift their perspective from asking "Why me?" to boldly declaring "What now?"

In their spare time, Kimberly and her husband enjoy the beauty of God's creation at their small lake house nestled on Table Rock Lake.

Connect with Kimberly:

KimberlyHaar.com

 @ KimberlyJHaar    @kimberly.haar    @KimberlyHaar

To get regular encouragement, tips, and additional resources to help you with your journey to growth and healing, join Kimberly's free email newsletter at KimberlyHaar.com.